THE POET'S CALLING

POETRY

Patmos and Other Poems (1955)
Third Day Lucky (1958)
Two Ballads of the Muse (1960)
Begging the Dialect (1960)
The Dark Window (1962)
A Valedictory Poem (1963)
An Irish Gathering (1964)
A Ballad of Billy Barker (1965)
Inscriptions (1967)
Because of This (1968)
The Hold of Our Hands (1968)
Selected Poems 1947-1967 (1968)
An Irish Album (1969)
Georges Zuk: Selected Verse (1969)
Answers (1969)
The Hunting Dark (1971)
Two Hundred Poems from the Greek Anthology (1971)
A Different Mountain (1972)
A Private Speech (1972)
Musebook (1972)
Three for Herself (1972)
Country Songs (1973)
Fools Wisdom (1974)
Timelight (1974)

BOOKS ABOUT POETRY

The Poetic Pattern (1956)
Poetry (1963)
The Practice of Poetry (1971)

EDITIONS OF POETRY

J. M. Synge: Collected Poems (1962)
Edward Thomas: Selected Poems (1962)
Selected Poems of Byron (1965)
David Gascoyne: Collected Poems (1965)
David Gascoyne: Collected Verse Translations (with Alan Clodd) (1970)

ANTHOLOGIES

Viewpoint: An Anthology of Poetry (1962)
Six Irish Poets (1962)
Poetry of the Thirties (1964)
Five Poets of the Pacific Northwest (1964)
Poetry of the Forties (1968)
The Cavalier Poets (1970)

THE POET'S CALLING

by

Robin Skelton

HEINEMANN
LONDON

BARNES & NOBLE
NEW YORK

Heinemann Educational Books Ltd
LONDON EDINBURGH MELBOURNE AUCKLAND TORONTO
HONG KONG SINGAPORE KUALA LUMPUR
IBADAN NAIROBI JOHANNESBURG
LUSAKA NEW DELHI

U.K. edition
ISBN 0 435 18819 4 (cased)
ISBN 0 435 18820 8 (paper)

U.S. edition
ISBN 0 06 496328 4 (cloth)
ISBN 0 06 496329 2 (paper)

Set in 11 on 12 Centaur

Published in Great Britain by
Heinemann Educational Books Ltd
48 Charles Street, London W1X 8AH
Published in the U.S.A. 1975 by
Harper & Row Publishers, Inc.
Barnes & Noble Import Division
Printed in Great Britain by
William Clowes & Sons, Limited
London, Beccles and Colchester

Contents

Acknowledgements

The author and publishers wish to thank the following for permission
to reprint copyright material: MacGibbon & Kee and Harcourt Brace
Jovanovich Inc for Poems 16 and 19 of 'Xaipe' and Poem 7 of 'One
Times One' from *Complete Poems* by e e cummings; Wesleyan Univer-
sity Press for 'Hallelujah: A Sestina' from *The Orb Weaver* by Robert
Francis and for 'Mirror Image: Port au Prince' from *Light and Dark* by
Barbara Howes; Basic Books Inc for extracts from *Poets on Poetry*, ed.
Howard Nemerov; Calder & Boyars Ltd for 'Revolver' by Alan
Riddell; Chatto & Windus and Harcourt Brace Jovanovich for
'Dissatisfaction with Metaphysics' and the note from *Collected Poems
of William Empson*; McGraw-Hill Book Company for the extracts from
The Glass House—The Life of Theodore Roethke by Allan Seager, copyright
1968 by Joan Seager, and for material copyrighted 1968 by Beatrice
Roethke in this book; Hugh MacDiarmid for 'A Moment in Eternity';
the Sterling Lord Agency for 'Ghost Tantras' and 'Poem' from *Ghost
Tantras*, copyright 1969; Washington Square Press, division of Simon
& Schuster Inc, for the extract from *Master Poems of the English Language*,
ed. Oscar Williams; Macmillan for 'The Winds Bastinado' from
Collected Poems by Edith Sitwell; Enitharmon Press and Kathleen Raine
for 'Faces of Day and Night' by Kathleen Raine; Charles Scribner's
Sons for 'Here' from *Words* by Robert Creeley, copyright 1967
Robert Creeley; the Regents of the University of California for the
extract from *The Creative Process*, ed. Brewster Ghiselin, originally
published by the University of California Press; Indiana University
Press for 'La Rose' by Paul de Vree from *Concrete Poetry: A World View*;
James Tate for 'Exposition' from *The Torches* by James Tate; Cambridge
University Press for the extract from *Inspiration and Poetry* by C. M.
Bowra; Teach Yourself Books Ltd for 'The Ball' and the extract from
Poetry by Robin Skelton; Robert Graves for the extracts from *Poetic
Craft and Principal* and *The Crowning Privilege*, and for 'A Bracelet' from
Poems 1965–1968; Yale University Press for 'Orpheus in Greenwich
Village' from *Views of Jeopardy* by Jack Gilbert; Mr Gavin Muir and
the Hogarth Press for the extract from *An Autobiography* by Edwin
Muir; Curtis Brown Ltd and Macmillan London and Basingstoke for
'Poem' from *Weep before God* by John Wain; *The Malahat Review*,

Acknowledgements

University of Victoria, British Columbia, for the Worksheets by Kingsley Amis on 'South', James K. Baxter 'The Jar', Anne Sexton 'Wallflower', Robert Francis 'The Hawk', and Robert Graves 'A Bracelet' from Nos. 4, 5, 6, 12 and 25, 1968–1973; Oxford University Press for 'Hill-Top and Guy Fawkes' from *Lodgers* by Tony Connor, for 'Poetic Objectivity' from *David Gascoyne Collected Verse Translations*, ed. Robin Skelton and Alan Clodd, and for 'The Curse' from *Collected Works Volume 1* by J. M. Synge; Oxford University Press and Liveright Publishing Corporation for the extract from *The Complete Poems and Selected Letters and Prose of Hart Crane*, ed. B. Weber; Chatto & Windus and Oxford University Press, New York, for 'New Hampshire, February' from *Collected Poems 1930–1960* by Richard Eberhart; Delacorte Press/Seymour Lawrence for 'Galileo Galilei' from *New and Selected Poems* by William Jay Smith; Macmillan & Co for the extracts from poems by W. B. Yeats; Faber & Faber Ltd and Doubleday & Co Inc for 'Where Knock is Open Wide' and 'I Need, I Need' from *The Collected Poems of Theodore Roethke*; Little Brown & Co for 'Skunk House' by Robert Lowell and extracts from *The Contemporary Poet as Artist and Critic* by Anthony Ostroff; Faber & Faber Ltd and Oxford University Press for 'The Sunlight on the Garden' from *The Collected Poems* by Louis MacNeice; Faber & Faber Ltd and Harper & Row for 'Crow's Song of Himself' from *Crow* by Ted Hughes, copyright 1971 by Ted Hughes.

It has not been possible in all cases to trace copyright holders of quoted extracts and poems. The publishers would be glad to hear from any such unacknowledged copyright holders.

Introduction

'What is it like to be a poet?' I am often asked this question, and I am always hard-put to find an answer, for I have been writing poems ever since I was a child and I cannot distinguish between my manhood and my poethood with any ease. Nevertheless the question, however crudely phrased, must be an important one if we consider poetry itself to be important, and so I find myself attempting an answer in this book.

During the past twenty years, and especially during the last decade, there have been quite a large number of publications in which the 'poetic experience' has been discussed. These have, mostly, been of two kinds. The first has consisted of examinations of the making of poetry and of the 'poetic trance', which, though usually involving some first-hand testimony from poets, has devoted the greater part of its attention to the presentation of explanation and theory. The second kind has consisted of interviews with poets or of comments by poets upon their own work. This second kind of book would seem to come close to telling us 'what it is like to be a poet' but it rarely does so, for the poets are usually occupied not in presenting instances of the poetic experience but in interpreting their actual work, commenting upon their attitudes to other poets, and giving background information; they are speaking, indeed, more as critics than as makers. Poets' autobiographies, with certain splendid exceptions, such as Edwin Muir's *Autobiography* and Howard Nemerov's subtle and haunting *Journal of a Fictive Life*, rarely deal with the heart of the matter; the majority of them could almost have been written by literary journalists, editors, or foreign correspondents. This is not very surprising, for most poets do have other literary concerns, and ones which are more productive of entertaining stories than is the solitary struggle of the imagination with an emerging poem. Moreover, most poets say all that they feel about poetry in their poems; they may even feel, like Walter de la Mare, that one cannot really discuss poetry except in the medium of poetry. Most poets also feel wary of exposing themselves to the risk of lying about poetic inspiration. It is so hard to be exact about such matters and it is, they feel strongly, downright dangerous to give a false impression, and thus to offend or alienate the Muse.

The concept of the Muse presents difficulties to many people. The word has archaic associations, and may even suggest a deliberately fanciful obscurantism on the part of the poet who uses the term. For many people it is simply a shorthand expression for the creative impulse, or for inspiration. For a large number of poets, however, the word has real meaning and almost awesome power. The Muse is the commanding force in the poet's life and requires continual attention, service, and honour.

Such a statement will strike some readers as an absurd inflation of reality. Some poets, even, may wince at it, and object to its romantic crudity, its melodramatic assertiveness. Nevertheless, that which some poets label as the 'muse experience' is central to poetic creation, and it is this experience which forces the poet to discipline his life in ways which non-poets may think peculiar.

I have used the word 'discipline' deliberately, for the popular picture of the poet is, I feel, that of a person who rejects the 'discipline' of social conformity and who frequently indulges in behaviour one might well characterize as anarchic. The popular picture of the poet is, of course, false; it is a caricature rather than a portrait. Unfortunately, many poets have, over the years, chosen to support popular misconceptions by becoming 'stage poets', as Irishmen frequently choose to entertain themselves and others by putting on the character of the 'stage Irishman'. Only other poets (and other Irishmen) are likely to perceive the spirit of irony in which the performance is conducted, and to understand that the manœuvre may be also a kind of self-protection. Not all poets (or Irishmen, or Scots, or Jews) choose to play this game, of course, but a sufficient number are always enough in evidence to perpetuate the entertaining fiction.

It must, however, be realized that some of the eccentricities popularly associated with poethood are not defensive or ironic affections but aspects of that discipline to which I have already referred, or consequences of that obsessive devotion to the Muse which rules the poet's social as well as his private behaviour. Each poet, however, discovers his own modus vivendi; he is obliged to come to terms with the Muse in his own way. Consequently, most poets are leery of making generalizations about the poetic experience; they are aware that, while the heart of the matter may be the same for all poets, almost everything else is likely to be different.

A book entirely about the poetic experience would be a valuable contribution to our understanding of some aspects of poetry if it were to be fully documented with details of the different approaches and attitudes of a large number of poets. Such a book, however, might strike the general reader as being too limited in its approach to answer that question 'What is it like to be a poet?' The general reader might, quite reasonably, wish to know something of the poet's relationship to his environment and his society. How can a poet earn his living without compromising his poetic integrity or dulling his sensibility? Can a poet, in the middle of the twentieth century, make a living from his art? Some readers concerned with the health of our culture might wish to learn of the difficulties poets face in a society organized in terms of other than poetic values. There are practical problems that all men must tackle; is the poet obliged to tackle them in a fashion that differs from that of the majority?

I have tried to answer some of these questions in this book, for I believe that they all direct our attention to the changing role of the poet in our Western society, and that it is important to scrutinize the role the artist plays in any culture. I have also tried to answer these questions in terms of the completely dedicated poet rather than in terms of the man of letters or teacher or journalist who writes poems from time to time, but who is not wholly committed by a sense of poetic vocation. Obviously, in doing this, I am making a series of highly personal judgements. Indeed, this book can hardly be other than a personal (and therefore biased) report. The greater part of my knowledge of the nature of poethood and of the poetic experience must derive from my own life. I have therefore been obliged to indulge in a certain amount of autobiography, though I have called other poets as witnesses to the truth or to the inadequacy of my own experience as often as possible. The testimonies of other poets have been gathered from conversations and by correspondence as well as from printed sources. I have chosen to limit my number of footnotes by only attaching them to quotations from published material. All statements that are presented without footnotes or other indications of previous publication appear in this book for the first time and have been passed for publication by the poets who made them. To those poets, and to the many students whose questions first set me to thinking of making this book, I must express my gratitude.

R.S.

ONE The Speckled Bird

During his trial for his life, Socrates spoke of his encounters with poets, and said:

> I presently recognized this, that what they composed they composed not by wisdom, but by nature and because they were inspired, like the prophets and givers of oracles; for these also say many fine things but know none of the things they say; it was evident to me that the poets too had experienced something of this same sort.[1]

Over two thousand and two hundred years later, Herbert Read stated:

> I can aver that all the poetry I have written which I continue to regard as authentic poetry was written immediately, instantaneously, in a condition of trance.[2]

Goethe, a hundred years earlier, told Eckermann

> They come and ask me what idea I meant to embody in my *Faust*; as if I knew myself and could inform them.[3]

Byron, perhaps remembering Socrates' words, told Thomas Moore

> A man's poetry is a distinct faculty, or Soul, and has no more to do with the everyday individual than Inspiration with the Pythoness when removed from her tripod.[4]

Not all poems are produced in an inspired state of mind or in a 'poetic trance', but the experience of this trance condition is a central fact in a poet's apprehension of his way of life. This is, indeed, the ideal act which, once it has occurred, becomes the goal of all poetic endeavour. C. M. Bowra has described the operation of Poetic inspiration very clearly:

---

[1] *Plato*, translated by H. N. Fowler. Heinemann 1914, Vol I, p. 85.
[2] Herbert Read, *Collected Essays in Literary Criticism*. Faber 1938, p. 110.
[3] *Conversations of Goethe with Eckermann*, translated by John Oxenford. Everyman Library 1935, p. 205.
[4] Thomas Moore (ed.), *Works of Lord Byron*. John Murray 1832–3, Volume V, p. 285.

The poet unaccountably finds himself dominated by something which absorbs his being and excludes other interests from his mind. It is not easy to define exactly what this is, but we may mark certain elements in it. Central to it is something which may be called an idea, though in some ways it is too vague to deserve the name. It has a powerful character and atmosphere of its own, and though at first it is too indefinite for intellectual analysis, it imposes itself on the poet with the majesty and authority of vision. Even if he does not fully understand it, he feels it and almost sees it. This is usually accompanied by words which fall into rhythmical patterns, sometimes without the poet knowing what they mean, though he is singularly attracted to them and cannot but make the most of them, confident that they will yield their meaning to him later. . . . This state is not static but dynamic, a source of vivid, almost violent activity. It begins at once to shoot out ideas of great force and intensity, and these are often accompanied by words which not only clarify them and relate them to the general scheme but are themselves of an unusual force and intensity. Inspiration sets to work with a will which nothing can withstand.

In many cases an idea may move faster than the words which pursue it, and the poet is hard put to keep abreast of it. We can see evidence for this in Pushkin's manuscripts. He will often write down complete lines and variant versions of them as if trying to catch the absolutely right effect, but no less often he will leave gaps and race after the next theme which lures him on, setting down a few odd words, a phrase or a rhyme or a mere clue to what he wishes to say. The whole thing seems to have been done at an extraordinary speed, as if the inspiring thoughts were often too fast for the words which pant after them. But so lively and powerful is the source of energy, so rich in suggestions and so actively at work in his consciousness, that he is able to come back to it and fill in the gaps later by reference to it. Though few poets work with Pushkin's speed and abundance, most know something like his condition. In this process, what begins by being almost unconscious becomes conscious; what is at the start an outburst of energy infused with a vague idea or an undifferentiated vision becomes concrete and definite; what is outside the poet's control is gradually made to submit to his will and judgement. Such, or something like it, seems to be the usual experience of poets, and such primarily inspiration is.[1]

The intensity of this experience can be almost overpowering. Dr Rosamund Harding in her *Anatomy of Inspiration* has listed a number of

[1] C. M. Bowra, *Inspiration and Poetry*. Cambridge University Press 1951, pp. 6–8.

instances of the way in which a poet's or artist's appearance may alter at such times:

The whole appearance and manner of the Pythoness underwent a change when exhausted with her struggles she finally sank beneath the power of the God. Something very like this happens when the creative process is at its height. Eye-witnesses have left descriptions of what they saw. Anton Schindler shall describe what Beethoven looked like when in his 'raptus'. Beethoven, as is known, was not remarkable in appearance; he was short and thick-set; his eyes were small and were almost hidden when he laughed. 'On the other hand,' Schindler says, 'they would suddenly be projected in unusual size, flashing as they rolled about, the pupils almost always turned upward, or immovable, staring down before them as soon as some idea had seized him. Therewith, however, his whole outward appearance would in the same way suddenly undergo a startling transformation, would assume a vividly inspired and imposing semblance, so that his slight figure, like his soul, would tower before one in gigantic size. These moments of sudden inspiration often would surprise him in the gayest company or in the street, and usually attracted the liveliest attention of all passers-by.' Mozart, also, was unimpressive in appearance, yet in moments of inspiration the artist within him became apparent in the change that came over his countenance. Schubert's friends knew by his 'flashing eye and altered tone of voice' when an idea had seized him. Wagner also has his 'raptus'. Weissheimer tells how once when he disturbed him when composing the Meistersinger, Wagner had opened the door and stood before him scarcely recognizable; 'his features were completely changed, almost wild.' Whoever had looked into Wagner's eyes would be unlikely to forget their mysterious expression. This changed appearance is not confined only to musicians. Medwin says of the school-boy Shelley when inspired: 'his eyes flashed, his lips quivered, his voice was tremulous with emotion, a sort of ecstasy came over him, and he talked more like a spirit or an angel than a human being.' D'Israeli tells an amusing story of the poet Gray when composing the 'Installation Ode':—'a friend calling on him, Gray flung open his door hastily, and in a hurried voice and tone exclaimed in the first verse of that Ode,

Hence, avaunt! 'tis holy ground!'

and D'Israeli says 'his friend started back at the disordered appearance of the bard, whose organism had disturbed his very air and countenance, till he had recovered himself.' Mrs Gaskell observed that Charlotte Brontë had peculiar eyes, 'large and well shaped; their colour a reddish brown. . . . The usual expression was of quiet listening intelligence; but now and then, on some occasion for vivid interest or wholesome indignation, a light would shine out, as if some spiritual lamp had been kindled . . . I never saw the like in any other human creature.'[1]

By no means all inspiration is of this degree of intensity. Sometimes the experience is of a deep inward calm, an almost dream-like suspension of ordinary feeling, in which and through which the poem is spoken as if by an inner voice. The poet Goethe referred to 'That undisturbed, direct manner of working, almost like a sleep-walker, which alone can lead to greatness'[2] and Coleridge to 'that state of nascent existence in the twilight of imagination and just on the vestibule of consciousness'.[3]

Brewster Ghiselin has described this calmer version of the poetic trance most successfully in two passages.

This state in no way involves or suggests irresolution. Paradoxically it often appears as an enhancement of certainty. It is as if the mind delivered from preoccupation with particulars were given into secure possession of its whole substance and activity. This yielding to the oceanic consciousness may be a distracting delight, which as Jacques Maritain has pointed out can divert the worker from formal achievement. In this extreme the experience verges upon the religious; but it is rarely so intense or so pure, and when it is, it is not often so enduring a preoccupation as to constitute a real threat to performance. More often it defines itself as no more than a sense of self-surrender to an inward necessity inherent in something larger than the ego and taking precedence over the established order. . . .

The concentration of such a state may be so extreme that the worker may seem to himself or others to be in a trance or some similar hypnotic or somnambulistic state. But actually the state of so-called trance so often mentioned as characteristic of the creative process or of stages in it differs markedly from ordinary trance or hypnosis, in its collectedness, its autonomy, its extreme watchfulness. And it seems never to be directly induced. It appears rather to be generated indirectly, to subsist as the characteristic of a consciousness partly unfocussed, attention diverted from the too-assertive contours of any particular scheme and dispersed upon an object without complete schematic representation. In short, the creative discipline when successful may generate a trance-

[1] Rosamond E. M. Harding, *An Anatomy of Inspiration*. Heffer 1948, pp. 20-21.

[2] Quoted in Clive Sansom (ed.), *The World of Poetry*. Phoenix House 1959, p. 104.

[3] ibid., p. 104.

like state, but one does not throw oneself into a trance in order to create.[1]

It must be emphasized that this experience feels 'natural' to the poet, whereas the more frenzied or manic experience of inspiration is so filled with energy as to appear more than natural. The difference is, perhaps, between walking a tightrope with absolute ease and confidence, the action being only the perfection of a natural capacity, and running at great speed up the vertical wall of a house, which, though a use of natural capacity, appears to have overcome all normal obstacles by the force of its own energy. Moreover, afterwards, the man on the roof of the house, like the poet staring down at the completed poem he cannot recall having controlled in any way (having been overmastered by energy, possessed of a daimon), cannot believe his own achievement.

When Keats said that 'if poetry comes not as naturally as the leaves to a tree it had better not come at all' he was speaking of the quieter form of trance, as was Rilke when he stated 'I must wait for the ringing in the silence, and I know that if I force the ringing, then it really won't come'.[2] Randall Jarrell in *Poetry and the Age* (1953), said 'A good poet is someone who manages, in a lifetime of standing out in thunderstorms, to be struck by lightning five or six times; a dozen or two dozen times and he is great.' Jarrell's metaphor is perhaps over-violent, but his remark does indicate that the poet is obliged to stand out in thunderstorms; he must contrive to place himself in a receptive position; he must be in a state of preparedness.

This state of preparedness has been described by a number of poets. Keats's version of it is the best known. He wrote to Richard Woodhouse on 27 October 1818:

A poet is the most unpoetical of any thing in existence; because he has no Identity he is continually informing and filling some other Body—the Sun, the Moon, the Sea, and Men and Women who are creatures of impulse are poetical and have about them an unchangeable attribute—the poet has none; no identity— he is certainly the most unpoetical of all God's creatures. . . . It is a wretched thing to confess; but it is a very fact that not one word I ever utter can be taken for granted as an opinion growing out of my identical nature—how can it, when I have no nature ? When I am in a room with People if I ever am free from speculating on creations of my own brain, then, not myself goes home

[1] Brewster Ghiselin (ed.), *The Creative Process*. Mentor Books 1955, pp. 15 and 25.
[2] Quoted in Sansom, op. cit., p. 107.

to myself; but the identity of everyone in the room begins to press upon me so that I am in a very little time annihilated—not only among men; it would be the same in a nursery of children. . . .[1]

The poet, in order to remain receptive, cannot afford to have fixed opinions or a fixed character. He may, of course, pretend to both when in company, but he is usually inwardly aware that this is simply a social manœuvre, like wearing a dress suit at a ball or putting on white flannels to play cricket. 'Poets—the best of them—' said Shelley 'are a very chameleonic race; they take the colour not only of what they feed on but of the very leaves under which they pass'.[2] Robert Frost described the necessary 'wise passiveness' (Wordsworth) or 'negative capability' (Keats) of the poet by saying 'Poets stick to nothing deliberately, but let what will stick to them, like burrs when they walk in the fields.'[3]

It is this necessary preparedness and watchfulness which makes many poets appear to be vague, dreamy, and absent-minded. Keats saw this watchfulness as essential. He wrote to Hessey on 9 October 1818 'The Genius of Poetry must work out its own salvation in a man. It cannot be matured by law and precept, but by sensation and watchfulness in itself.'[4]

This is, however, only one aspect of that state of preparedness in which the poet must attempt continually to live. It is not enough to remain receptive, watchful, poised to receive the lightning bolt; it is not enough to spend one's time waiting, like Matthew Arnold's Scholar Gypsy, for 'the spark from heaven to fall'. One must learn to turn oneself into a lightning conductor and to attract the visitation of the Muse. Every poet has a different method of doing this. A. E. Housman described his own procedure in a well-known passage:

> Having drunk a pint of beer at luncheon—beer is a sedative to the brain, and my afternoons are the least intellectual portion of my life— I would go out for a walk of two or three hours. As I went along, thinking of nothing in particular, only looking at things around me and following the progress of the seasons, there would flow into my mind, with sudden and unaccountable emotion, sometimes a line or two of verse, sometimes a whole stanza at once, accompanied, not preceded,

[1] Lord Houghton, *Life and Letters of John Keats*. Everyman's Library 1927, p. 134.

[2] Quoted in Sansom, op. cit., p. 89.

[3] ibid., p. 89.

[4] Lord Houghton, *Life and Letters of John Keats*. Everyman's Library 1927, p. 130.

by a vague notion of the poem which they were destined to form part
of. Then there would usually be a lull of an hour or so, then perhaps
the spring would bubble up again. I say bubble up, because, so far as I
could make out, the source of the suggestions thus proffered to the brain
was an abyss which I have already had occasion to mention, the pit of
the stomach. When I got home I wrote them down, leaving gaps, and
hoping that further inspiration might be forthcoming another day.
Sometimes it was, if I took my walks in a receptive and expectant
frame of mind; but sometimes the poem had to be taken in hand and
completed by the brain, which was apt to be a matter of trouble and
anxiety, involving trial and disappointment, and sometimes ending in
failure. I happen to remember distinctly the genesis of the piece which
stands last in my first volume. Two of the stanzas, I do not say which,
came into my head, just as they are printed, while I was crossing the
corner of Hampstead Heath between the Spaniard's Inn and the foot-
path to Temple Fortune. A third stanza came with a little coaxing after
tea. One more was needed, but it did not come: I had to turn to and
compose it myself, and that was a laborious business. I wrote it
thirteen times, and it was more than a twelvemonth before I got it
right.[1]

Trelawny said of Shelley 'He told me that he always wrote best in the
open air, in a boat, under a tree, or on the bank of a river.'[2] Milton
found the very early morning the best time to write, as does William
Stafford. Burns preferred the twilight. The poet must, in other words,
discover the situation or time of day in which he can experience the
creative mood most easily, and arrange his life around this discovery. He
may even find that he can help himself by a process of self-conditioning.
If he habitually uses a certain place, or object, or wears a particular piece
of clothing when writing, there is a possibility that he can 'switch on'
with the aid of these. Some poets always wear the same old coat when
sitting down to write. Dumas wrote his poems only on yellow paper.
Pierre Jean Jouve used a certain armchair. Many poets have one particular
pen which they use for poetry and for nothing else; the act of picking up
this particular pen can set the creative mood as was the case with
Southey. These are minor manœuvres, easily managed. Some poets,
however, find themselves obliged to perform more elaborate rituals.

This attempt at creating for oneself a 'conditioned reflex' attached to

[1] A. E. Housman, *The Name and Nature of Poetry*. Cambridge University Press
1939, pp. 49–50
[2] E. J. Trelawny, *Records of Shelley, Byron and the Author*. B. M. Pickering 1878,
Vol I, p. 104.

particular objects or places is not merely an endeavour to trigger off a particular mood of receptivity or imaginative activity, it is also an attempt to control one's environment and organize a particular kind of solitude. If, as one sits down to write, one is too aware of one's surroundings, of distant noises in the house, of unfamiliar objects recently added to one's room, one can find that the mind begins to wander idly and play upon the surface of things. But if the environment is, as it were, dominated by a small number of objects which one has always associated with the making of poems, then the other objects dwindle into insignificance. It is important to be able to withdraw into a purposive solitude. Rilke said in his *Letters to a Young Poet*:

> What is needed is, in the end, simply this: solitude, great inner solitude. Going into yourself and meeting no one for hours on end—that is what you must be able to attain. To be alone, as you were alone in childhood, when the grown-ups were going about, involved with things which seemed important and great, because the great ones looked so busy and because you grasped nothing of their business.[1]

This solitude does not have to be a physical one. A poet can, if he practises, learn to achieve this solitude in many situations. He can withdraw into himself in a crowded room, in the street, in a bar or restaurant. I myself am blessedly short-sighted so that I can, when in a bar or restaurant, isolate myself from all visual interruptions by taking off my glasses. I find, indeed, that a noisy room, when the noise is so pervasive as to lack all definite characteristics, and when the people in the room are all busy about their own affairs and unknown to me, can provide an admirable solitude. Moreover, in such an environment, there can be no claims made upon me. If the telephone rings I know the call is not for me. If there is an argument I am not required to join or settle it. I have no responsibilities.

Poets have often been regarded as irresponsible people, forgetful of their families, careless over practicalities, and selfish in the extreme. It must be admitted that there is some truth in this. The poet will do his best to avoid anything which threatens his poethood. Walter de la Mare has said 'Again and again he must stand back from the press of habit and convention. He must keep on recapturing solitude.'[2] The poet will, moreover, if he can manage it, so organize his domestic arrangements that everything and everyone around him supports him in his vocation.

---

[1] Quoted in Sansom, op. cit., p. 122.
[2] ibid., p. 122.

He may, like Pope, build himself a secluded workroom or studio and forbid interruption by anyone save in life or death emergencies. He may, like Wordsworth, press his nearest and dearest into the service of the Muse and make use of his sister's journals. He may, like Milton, make his wife into an amanuensis, or even quite simply absent himself from his family for long periods. He is likely to make absurd and impractical demands, to spend money he cannot afford on buying some object he feels would help to stimulate his imagination, a picture, an objet d'art, a vellum-bound folio, hi-fi equipment. All this he will do with bland assurance that nobody could reasonably object to his selfishness for to him it is not selfishness at all; it is part of his performance of his vocation. There are even instances of poets bringing their mistresses home to meet their wives, convinced by the intensity of their belief that what excites them to poetry cannot be anything but admirable, into assuming that no-one else can possibly object to something so clearly sensible and practical.

All this, of course, may seem to suggest that the poet is something of a monster, and that he would say with Dickens's Harold Skimpole: 'You know I don't intend to be responsible. I never could do it. Responsibility is a thing that has always been above me—or below me.'[1]

The difference between Harold Skimpole and the poet is obvious. Skimpole's selfishness and ruthlessness is entirely self-indulgent; he pursues pleasure and avoids all occasions of unpleasantness. The poet, however, does not shelve responsibilities or demand the patronage or support of others in order to pursue pleasure, but in order to free himself to devote all his energies to the making of poems which may frequently cause him much agony of mind and even lead him to the edge of emotional breakdown and to total exhaustion. It was this which caused Yeats to cry in his poem, *All Things Can Tempt Me*

> (I) would be now, could I but have my wish,
> colder and dumber and deafer than a fish[2]

There *are* Skimpoles in the world of poetry, of course. There are Skimpoles in every artistic community, for the possession of an 'artistic sensibility' can often be used as an excuse for anti-social selfishness. Most poets are keenly aware of this, and frequently find themselves suspecting a Skimpole in themselves. They ask themselves if their poetry

[1] Charles Dickens, *Bleak House*, Chapter LXI.
[2] Peter Allt and Russell K. Alspach (eds.), *The Variorum Edition of the poems of W. B. Yeats*. The Macmillan Company 1957, p. 267.

is important enough to justify the way in which they disrupt the lives of their families. They wonder if they should not devote more time to earning money, to advancing themselves in their non-poetic careers. Frequently harassed by these doubts and by guilt they find that they are too troubled to achieve poetry at all. Many, indeed, as family responsibilities increase, and growing children require more financial outlay, are unable to write more than occasionally. Moreover, the pressures of modern Western Society upon the individual are numerous and frequent. It is difficult for a poet to survive, to retain that condition of emotional and intellectual receptivity, that concentrated yet impersonal awareness, which is essential to him, and it is hard for him to preserve that store of psychic energy which he needs to cope with the situation when the lightning strikes. Stefan Zweig in 1943 wrote worriedly, 'I ask myself repeatedly, with a kind of private anxiety: will it be possible for such personalities, completely devoted to the lyric art, to exist in our time, in our new forms of life, which drive men out murderously from all inner contemplation as a forest fire drives wild animals from their hidden lairs?'[1] Kathleen Raine, answering a questionnaire in 1946, admitted 'I write poems when all my other work is up to date, and I am not working against time for money. This happens much too seldom. But I know I ought to put poetry first and that economic worries ought not to deter me. It is a weakness.' In answer to another question she wrote, 'I intended, even as a child, to be a poet, but have not always remembered my vocation. I am weak and allow people to make too many claims on my time, and lack the necessary ruthlessness to do what I know I should do.'[2] Yeats, struggling with similar difficulties, once laid his curse

> on plays
> That have to be set up in fifty ways,
> On the day's war with every knave and dolt,
> Theatre business, management of men.[3]

Clive Sansom commented in 1959

Every poet today—in fact, everyone with any sense of vocation—has to decide how far, for him, the demands of society may be met and

---

[1] Quoted in Sansom, op. cit., pp. 124–125.
[2] Kathleen Raine, *A Question of Poetry*. Richard Gilbertson 1967, p. (1).
[3] *The Fascination of What's Difficult*, in Peter Allt and Russell K. Alspach (eds.), *The Variorum Edition of the Poems of W. B. Yeats*. The Macmillan Company 1957, p. 260.

turned to account, and at what point they become a menace to be skillfully avoided or passionately resisted.[1]

Unfortunately the poet is not merely obliged to achieve a condition of sustained receptivity, to remain continually sensitized and aware, but also to labour. 'Without unceasing Practice nothing can be done' said Blake, that most inspired and visionary of all poets, and 'Practice is Art. If you leave off you are lost.'[2] Shelley, writing to Medwin, said, 'The source of poetry is native and involuntary, but requires severe labour in its development.'[3] Goethe wrote to Roderer in 1772, 'The artist who is not also a craftsman is no good.'[4] The poet who does not practise his craft, develop his technical skill, explore new methods and new subtleties of diction, structure, and imagery, is not adequately prepared to receive the moment of inspiration. The poet, moreover, must not only practise the conscious craft, but also practise the use of his imagination; he must labour to improve perception as well as expression. The majority of his poems will not be wholly 'given'; they will have to be laboured after and, though there will usually be some 'given' material in any poem worthy of the name, it may not provide more than a small part of the whole. Herbert Read was exceptional in finding only his totally inspired poems acceptable. T. S. Eliot maintained that while some parts of all his poems were 'given' he was by no means sure that they were always the best parts, and he was sure that no reader could distinguish the inspired passages from those resulting from more conscious labour. The poet must, indeed, so perfect and discipline his mind and sensibility that he can come close to the most intense and original poetic vision without being more than intermittently dependent upon the sudden surprising information, the flash of brilliant intuition. It is impossible for any poet to compose a poem of substantial length if he is totally dependent upon the descent of the lightning; only the purely lyric poet can, perhaps, afford to rely almost wholly upon the Muse. The rest of us must learn to use our wits, and steer ourselves into a state of mind so close to the 'poetic trance' that we can make use of intuitive perceptions without being wholly dependent upon them.

The pursuit of poetry thus demands considerable discipline and demands the learning of skills which, though known when experienced,

[1] Sansom, op. cit., p. 125.
[2] Quoted in Sansom, op. cit., p. 112.
[3] Quoted in Sansom, op. cit., p. 112.
[4] ibid., p. 114.

cannot easily be described. The poet is thus in the unhappy position of one who is unable ever satisfactorily to explain his procedures and his necessities to anyone who has not written poetry with a similar degree of awareness. Although his vocation demands a special way of life, it is a way of life that cannot be described in terms of rules or rituals, for each poet must create his own order. Although the strains and pressures upon him are so numerous and often so severe that he risks mental breakdown, the general laiety are liable to see the mental instability as rather the cause than the consequence of poetic vocation. It is not perhaps surprising that when W. B. Yeats wrote his autobiographical novel he called it *The Speckled Bird,* remembering that verse in Isaiah

> My soul is as the speckled bird: all the
> birds of heaven are against it.

TWO The Child and the Muse

It has been said that poets are born, not made. On the other hand, a great many biographies and autobiographies of poets tend to suggest that there are common factors in the childhood of almost all of those who are later regarded as poets. From this it may be deduced that there is a certain kind of early experience which makes a boy or girl grow up to be a poet. It is, however, only fair to point out that the deduction may be false, for many children who appear to have had the same childhood conditioning as the poets do not turn to poetry, and some of the future poets' childhood experiences might just as reasonably be regarded as the consequence as the cause of a poetic sensibility.

We have few details of the childhood of poets before the nineteenth century brought a fashion for autobiography and the first stirrings of modern psychology made people aware of the significance and interest of childhood experience. If we think of the childhood of the Romantic poets we can find a number of common factors. Coleridge told Thomas Poole that as a young child he was 'fretful and timorous' and that 'the schoolboys drove me from play, and were always tormenting me, and hence I took no pleasure in boyish sports, but read incessantly'. He tells Poole:

> I found the Arabian Nights' Entertainments, one tale of which (the tale of a man who was compelled to seek for a pure virgin) made so deep an impression on me (I had read it in the evening while my mother was mending stockings), that I was haunted by spectres, whenever I was in the dark: and I distinctly remember the anxious and fearful eagerness with which I used to watch the window in which the books lay, and whenever the sun lay upon them, I would seize it, carry it by the wall, and bask and read. My father found out the effect which these books had produced, and burnt them.
>
> So I became a *dreamer*, and acquired an indisposition to all bodily activity; and I was fretful, and inordinately passionate, and as I could not play at anything, and was slothful, I was despised and hated by the boys; and because I could read and spell and had, I may truly say, a

13

memory and understanding forced into almost an unnatural ripeness, I was flattered and wondered at by all the old women.[1]

Wordsworth's childhood solitude, and his love of wandering and dreaming are too well known to require comment. It is, however, interesting to note that, according to Mary Moorman, he also had a passion for the Arabian Nights. Wordsworth's father was often away from home and the boy was much attached to his mother. Coleridge's father died suddenly just before the poet's tenth birthday. Keats' father died when the poet was nine years old; Keats also was passionately devoted to his mother, who died when he was only fifteen years old. The boy, normally high-spirited, pugnacious, and athletic, according to Lord Houghton, 'hid himself in a nook under the master's desk for several days, in a long agony of grief, and would take no consolation from master or friend'.[2] Byron's father separated from his mother when the boy was two years old, and the child's earliest years were dominated by his mother who alternately spoiled and tormented him. Shelley was brought up with his sisters until he was seven or eight and had little to do with his father; though he later became known for pugnacity he was, like Coleridge, uninterested in the usual games of boyhood. Landor appears to have found it difficult to understand his father, but was devoted to his mother and elder sister. Like Keats, he was an athletic and pugnacious boy. John Clare's mother was his chief source of imaginative stimulus; she told him many stories of 'Witches' dread powers and fairy feats' and was eager that her only son should become a scholar. If we survey the early life of Tennyson, Wilde, and Yeats, we come across a similar pattern. The father is often absent from home or remote; the mother or some other woman is the boy's chief instructor and influence.

All this could, of course, mean little. The young child is always dependent on its mother, and the father of a family is often slightly at a loss with young children or busy with his work. Moreover, not every child with an absent father and an imaginative mother turns into an artist or poet. Nevertheless, the frequency with which this particular pattern turns up in the lives of the poets does suggest that it may have some bearing upon our problem. It may, however, be thought that this pattern is peculiar to the nineteenth century when fathers were ordinarily somewhat more inclined than we are to leave their children entirely in the

[1] Kathleen Raine (ed.), *The Letters of Samuel Taylor Coleridge*. Grey Walls Press 1950, p. 7.
[2] Lord Houghton, op. cit., p. 12.

hands of the womenfolk. Constantine Fitzgibbon describes Dylan Thomas's father as 'rather remote' and tells how the poet's mother 'pampered and coddled' the weakly child. He reports 'The distance between his sister and himself was such that in practice he was an only child. His home life was thus a solitary one, and this solitude was made the greater by the loneliness of the sick-bed.'[1]

Edith Sitwell said in her autobiography, *Taken Care Of*, 'My parents were strangers to me from the day of my birth' and tells us, 'As a child and a very young girl, I spent a good deal of time with my two grandmothers.'[2] She learned to read before she was four years old, and her childhood was filled with solitary dreaming. According to Allan Seager, Theodore Roethke 'seems to have remembered his father as a stern, short-tempered man whose love he doubted'.[3] Tony Connor's father left home when his son was four years old and was not heard of again until his death thirty years later. Robert Graves wrote in *Goodbye to All That*:

My father being a very busy man, an inspector of schools for the Southwark district of London, we children saw practically nothing of him except during the holidays. Then he behaved very sweetly, and told us stories with the formal beginning, not 'once upon a time', but always: 'And so the old gardener blew his nose on a red pocket handkerchief. . . .' He occasionally played games with us, but for the most part, when not busy with educational work, was writing poems, or being president of literary or temperance societies. My mother, kept busy running the household and conscientiously carrying out her social obligations as my father's wife, did not see so much of us as she would have liked, except on Sundays or when we happened to be ill. We had a nurse, and one another, and found that companionship sufficient.[4]

Robert Creeley's father died when the boy was two years old. Patrick Creagh and John Montague were both brought up by aunts. Anthony Hecht and T. S. Eliot both found their fathers remote creatures. Kathleen Raine found her father unsympathetic and remote. Jeni Couzyn said of hers, 'I almost felt that he was an absent father, and it was only as an adult that I was able to form a relationship with him at all' and added,

[1] Constantine FitzGibbon, *The Life of Dylan Thomas*. J. M. Dent 1965, pp. 24 and 40.

[2] Edith Sitwell, *Taken Care Of, An Autobiography*. Hutchinson 1966, pp. 27 and 59.

[3] Allan Seager, *The Glass House: The Life of Theodore Roethke*. McGraw-Hill 1968, p. 26.

[4] Robert Graves, *Goodbye to All That*.

'Now I flip through my little notebook of all my poet friends I think this has been true of most of them.'

Though all this suggests a pattern, it would be unwise to regard it as more than one element in the whole picture. Thinking back over my own childhood it is not the relative remoteness of my father which seems central to my experience, but my solitude. An only child in a small village, the son of the schoolmaster, I had few friends when small. My time was divided between solitary wanderings and the creation of elaborate dramas with my toys, and long walks with my mother, who read me stories and poems, and who introduced me to the delights of picking blackberries, and to beachcombing, and who, when I was very small, and a little frightened of the water, simply and efficaciously conquered my hesitations by dunking me with almost ritual decisiveness in the sea. My mother, like the mother of Clare, and the mothers of many poets was, and is, a highly intuitive and imaginative woman; I learned, I think, from her to relish the strange, admire the lovely, and be aware of the inner world of intuition and imagination. My dependence upon my own thoughts and dreams for my entertainment and comfort was increased by the bullying of the other boys at the village school; for one period of many weeks I was permitted no playtime but locked up in the coke-shed for the whole period of the mid-morning break, and left there in the dust and pitch blackness to listen to the shouts and laughter outside my prison. At my boarding school, perhaps because the habit of solitude had grown ingrained, I was also lonely. A skinny and unathletic child, I was bullied there also, and spent much time alone either reading or, on Sundays, wandering the countryside and the fields round the school. It is easy in retrospect to exaggerate. I had some friends, obviously. Though bad at games, once I became large enough not to be a victim, I was left alone by all but my most devoted enemies, and in the holidays I enjoyed companionship with other boys and, on rare though splendid occasions, that of my father.

In my own life, therefore, I can see a similar pattern to that presented by the lives of many other poets. It was, however, the habit of solitude which, I believe, set me first to feeling a compulsion to write poetry. I would believe if I could, perhaps, that it was my vocation as a poet that led me to embrace solitude, but I cannot comfortably make that claim. I can, however, state that from the age of eight years (my earliest surviving manuscript was written when I was eight years and five months old) poetry was an essential part of my life, and that at the age of eleven I determined to become a poet.

It is not uncommon for the desire to become a poet to afflict children at this age. Kathleen Raine 'intended, even as a child, to be a poet'.[1] Pope tells us that he wrote verse as a small child, saying, 'I lisp'd in numbers, for the numbers came.'[2] Many children write poems, and the juvenilia of famous poets is often not noticeably better than that of many children who never grow to be writers. My own childhood poems are, indeed, a good deal worse than the majority of children's poems I have seen. What is it that causes some children of a solitary and introspective temperament and with a vivid imagination and rich fantasy life to become poets when others do not ?

Here we approach matters which are difficult to discuss with any precision. It seems that the solitary, imaginative child devoted to poetry and susceptible to experiences of the 'poetic trance' is likely to experience between the ages of twelve and fifteen (though sometimes earlier, sometimes later) something we must call a 'vision'. Robert Graves told his Oxford audience in 1965:

One fine summer evening, at the age of twelve, I was sitting on an iron roller behind the school cricket pavilion, with nothing much in my head, when I received a sudden celestial illumination: It occurred to me that I knew *everything*. I remember letting my mind range rapidly over all its familiar subjects of knowledge; only to find that this was no foolish fancy. I *did* know everything. To be plain: though conscious of having come less than a third of the way along the path of formal education, and being weak in mathematics, shaky in French grammar, and hazy about English history, I nevertheless held the key of truth in my hand, and could use it to open any lock of any door. Mine was no religious or philosophical theory, but a simple method of looking sideways at disorderly facts so as to make perfect sense of them.

I slid down from the roller, wondering what to do with my embarrassing gift. Whom could I take into my confidence ? Nobody. Even my best friends would say 'You're mad,' and either send me to Coventry or organize my general scragging, or both. It occurred to me that perhaps I had better embody the formula in a brief world message, circulated anonymously to the leading newspapers. In that case I should have to work under the bedclothes after dark, by the light of a flash-lamp, and use the cypher I had recently perfected. But I remembered my broken torch-light bulb, and the difficulty of replacing it until the next day. No: there was no immediate hurry. I had everything

[1] Kathleen Raine, *A Question of Poetry*. Richard Gilbertson 1967, p. (i).
[2] Alexander Pope, *Epistle to Dr Arbuthnot*, l. 128.

securely in my head. Again I experimented; and again the doors opened smoothly. Then the school-bell rang from a distance, calling me to preparation and prayers.

Early next day I awoke to find that I still had a fairly tight grasp of my secret; but a morning's lessons intervened, and when I then locked myself into the privy, and tried to record my formula on the back of an old exercise book, my mind went too fast for my pen, and I began to cross out—a fatal mistake—and presently crumpled up the page and pulled the chain on it. That night I tried again under the bedclothes, but the magic had evaporated and I could get no further than the introductory sentence.

My vision of truth did not recur, though I went back a couple of times to sit hopefully on the roller; and before long doubts tormented me—gloomy doubts about a great many hitherto stable concepts, such as the authenticity of the Gospels, the perfectibility of man, and the absoluteness of the Protestant moral code. All that survived was an after-glow of the bright light in my head, and the certainty that it had been no delusion. This is still with me, for I now realize that what overcame me that evening was a sudden awareness of the power of intuition, the supra-logic that cuts out all routine processes of thought and leaps straight from problem to answer. I did not in fact know everything, but became aware that in moments of real emergency the mind can weigh an infinite mass of imponderables and make immediate sense of them. This is how poems get written.

I have since found that this mystic experience is not at all an uncommon one. Something like one person in twenty has enjoyed it and I am convinced that the original moment, when Adam and Eve first looked at each other in wonder under the moon and signalled 'We are We', was an experience of the same sort, complementarily enjoyed by both; their foretaste of ultimate wisdom.[1]

Later, he told an interviewer for *The Paris Review*

You probably had a similar vision, and you've forgotten it. It needn't be a vision of anything; so long as it's a foretaste of Paradise. Blake had one. All poets and painters who have that extra 'thing' in their work seem to have had this vision and never let it be destroyed by education. Which is all that matters.[2]

This 'foretaste of Paradise' can be experienced either once or several times and can take many forms. Robert Sward experienced it at the age of eighteen while serving in the U.S. Navy. While walking the deck

[1] Robert Graves, *Poetic Craft and Principle*. Cassell 1967, pp. 136–8.
[2] *The Paris Review*, Number 47, p. 138.

alone he was suddenly overcome by a sense of illimitable radiant power and total understanding of all the forces of the Universe. He was even convinced momentarily that he could fly. I remember a number of such experiences; they usually took place in solitude in a wood or, once, on a lonely beach. In my case these experiences were of total communion with the forces of the earth and of nature; it seemed as if I had taken on a knowledge that made me one with the universe. John Montague has described this vision of total understanding as 'the Divine Sophia', 'the experience of the Universe of Light'. Discussing the whole matter he said:

> There are two things mixed up here. There are two primary experiences in the formation of the poetic psyche. I say two primary ones but there are lots of other experiences as well. One is the experience of the Universe of Energies, of the earth as a ball, as something that you're on. This can come quite early. I once tracked down when it happened to me but I prefer to keep that secret. This kind of light as to the whole, this illumination as to the power of the Universe upon which you move, can be seen also in terms of a concrete figure, like the Apollo whom Mr Graves chooses to deny, who in Celtic Myth would be something like the stag-headed God, a figure of total understanding. The *Collected Poems* of MacDiarmid[1] open with this vision. It is also the end of Dante. It is the supreme experience of knowledge.

John Montague, talking further of the development of the poetic faculty said:

> The growth of a poet is, of course, entangled with one's growth as a man. I can remember certain experiences which are very deeply buried in me. One—very early on—seven, eight, nine perhaps—was the experience of the finiteness of the body, and the spirit trapped in the body and reciting in the darkness 'I am I and I must die, the little body'. This went on for me for about three or four months.

This childhood experience of mortality appears to be common with poets and artists. Another friend of mine has said that almost all the writers he knows came near to death at a certain point in their childhood, often by drowning. I remember this happening to myself. I had gone down for the fourth time and when I came up I was extremely waterlogged, and found myself, as in a dream, simply abandoning the body as an irrelevant and outworn thing. It was an intense, but, curiously, not really frightening

---

[1] MacDiarmid's Poem, *A Moment of Eternity*, appeared in his first collection, *Annals of the Five Senses*, in 1923, and is reprinted on pp. 208–212.

experience once I had resigned myself, as I did, to what appeared almost inevitable. At that time I experienced quite distinctly that dialogue between the soul and the body which has been the subject of so many poems.

Other dialogues also have occurred to me, as to many other poets in their childhood and adolescence. I say 'dialogue' for frequently the tree, or rock, or wood to which I spoke appeared to be answering me, though sometimes in a language of silence that I could only dimly apprehend. Those poems in which poets apostrophize the moon, or the sea, or a tree, or even, as in the case of Burns, a mouse, are not the fantasies, or even quite the soliloquies, that most readers believe them to be. They are frequently accurate records of an experience of communication, of dialogue, that is central to certain kinds of poetic sensibility. John Montague has told me of one such experience of his own:

> I remember once, writing one of my earliest poems at home in the farmhouse, and going out for a walk I remember walking up the hill behind the house—we had some fir trees at the top, the only firs there were around,—and I came out on the little head and I saw the moon, the full moon, and I had a dialogue with her. This would have been in early adolescence. And it keeps coming back; I think it has come back into my work. In *Tides* she came back. She did the same thing. She reappeared at a crucial moment of my life. I looked out of a window, and there she was, streaming in her light through onto a woman's body which had become almost like a fish's or become silver or . . . The power of the moon as the great silent female guardian of part of the world.

This is, of course, a vision of the Muse, of the female principle, of Anima, of the White Goddess. The Muse is, however, also the Earth Mother, and one can easily refer experiences of intense communion with the natural world to her. John Montague reported:

> I remember another episode in my youth which I find very strange and which still occupies, haunts me. As a boy I was not lonely, but I was very much alone. And this business of wandering through the hills and with my dogs endlessly exploring little creeks, little rivers, discovering wells, thorny patches. There was one small wood, which is not really a wood, a kind of thicket—overlooking a river and in very early puberty I used to go there and I used to take off all my clothes slowly and I used to get into the trees and swing from tree to tree with my body very excited, then drop from the trees into the soft mud below until I was covered with mud and then go down and wash in the river.

This almost ritual embrace of the earth has parallels in the experience of many other poets. John Clare described an experience of his early childhood, when he was only five or six, when he approached an intuition of the mysterious power and authority of the natural world.

> I had often seen the large heath called Emmonsales stretching its yellow furze from my eyes into unknown solitudes . . . and my curiosity urgd me to steal an opportunity to explore it that morning I had imagind that the world's end was at the orizon and that a day's journey was able to find it so I went on with my heart full of hope's pleasures and discoverys expecting when I got to the brink of the world that I coud look down like looking into a large pit and see into its secrets the same as I believd I coud see heaven by looking into the water . . . So I eagerly wanderd on & rambled along the furze the whole day till I got out of my knowledge when the very wild flowers seemd to forget me . . . often wondering to myself that I had not found the edge the sky still touchd the ground in the distance & my childish wisdom was puzzld . . . when I got home I found my parents in the greatest distress & half the village about hunting me. . . .[1]

e. e. cummings recorded his own first encounter with these mysteries. In his *six nonlectures* (1953) he wrote:

> Here as a very little child, I first encountered the mystery who is Nature; here my enormous smallness entered Her illimitable being; and here someone actually infinite or impossibly alive—someone who might almost (but not quite) have been myself—wanderingly wandered the mortally immortal complexities of Her beyond imagining imagination. . . .
> The wonder of my first meeting with Herself is with me now; and also with me is the coming (obedient to Her each resurrection) of a roguish and resistless More Than Someone: Whom my deepest selves unfailingly recognized, though His disguise protected him from all the world.[2]

Sometimes this experience of sudden illumination, of sudden communication with the world of Nature brings with it a sense of the underlying completeness and perfection of existence. Kathleen Raine wrote in 1946

> Certain experiences are absolute in themselves. Truth or illusion, we have from time to time the conviction that certain things exist, in

[1] John and Anne Tibble, *John Clare, His Life and Poetry*. Heinemann 1956, p. 12.

[2] e.e. cummings, *six nonlectures*.

themselves, with the completeness that we seek constantly in all works of art, to imitate. My earliest experience of that entity was of flowers; an experience childish in itself, but worth examining, because the illusion of reality is one that concerns an adult no less than a child, and an artist continually.

Can I convey exactly what, when I first remember them—at three years old, or possibly younger still—flowers were? I was standing looking up at some dark red hollyhocks, growing in front of the wooden fence of my parents' garden, that I had never been beyond. I know that something was behind the hollyhocks, not only a wooden fence, but a world that went on and on, without ever coming to the end of itself. It was simply the world, and it was there, all of it, no matter what. This knowledge was not at all frightening, for in any case the world was beyond the hollyhocks, and I in front of them. They were the here and now, the world was everywhere else. But from that world beyond, extending from my flower to everywhere and everything beyond, from the sky and the day, the sunshine flooded, and shone and glittered upon the dark red petals. I have seen that same light since, that was reflected from the glossy ridges of the hollyhock petals, upon many other surfaces; upon the glossy wings of flies; upon the spokes of bicycle wheels, and the windscreens of motor-cars; upon glass dishes on hot days; upon the Thames, crossing the river from Charing Cross, as the train passes the Lion brewery, and the river bursts into view; upon innumerable blades of grass, in the dry summer; upon brass, water, old tins on rubbish-dumps; no matter where, for it is everywhere, the golden light of the sun itself.

So the light shone on the deep red flower petals at which I looked. I was a very small child, but my white starched pinafore and blue hair-ribbons I took for granted, as I did the world that lay beyond the flower. That I, or the world, might be a variable, I did not know, nor did it concern me, for the experience of the flower was a constant absolute, and complete thing in itself.

The flower was a face, a statement. A statement of what? Only of itself, as music states itself, as a painting states itself. What is a statement, a painting, or a piece of music, of? What is a flower of? The flower is absolute, like Mona Lisa or the Sphinx, those riddles that are their own answers. Flowers were, for me, a first experience and knowledge of things in themselves perfect, of the faces, one might say, with which the world looks at us, and we at the world's face. Those grave, still, smiling faces of nature itself, who does not know them? And yet, in what sense is a flower more an entity than a stem, or a root? How does it come that they carry conviction, as if they were eternal things?[1]

[1] Kathleen Raine, *Faces of Day and Night*. Enitharmon Press 1972, pp. 6–8.

Such experiences as these are not restricted to poets, of course. Most adolescents with any degree of sensitivity experience similar happenings, and all are, at one time or another, haunted by dreams and intimations which disturb them with a feeling that they have, for a little space, 'seen into the life of things'. The difference between the poet and the non-poet appears to be simply that the effect upon the former is lasting, while the latter soon forgets or dismisses the experience. It is obvious that for some people certain events are formative or seminal, while the same events may have little lasting effect upon others. Nevertheless I must make the point that the majority of poets appear to have had not one, but several of these experiences, and that the memory of them, and their recurrence in later life, is seen by them as relating directly to the nature of their poethood.

There is one vision which is not uncommon among poets but rare in others, and this is the vision of the Muse. John Montague's moon-dialogue is clearly one of these, for the moon was felt to be a feminine presence, a goddess, and e.e. cummings' vision was of Nature as the Goddess. One of my own was even more precise in its imagery. I was in my early adolescence—I cannot remember the exact date—when one morning, lying in my bed between sleep and waking, I saw a vision of a girl. If it was a dream it was of such intensity that the image persisted in phantom fashion for seconds after I was fully awake. This girl was blonde, grey-eyed, beautiful, and her features resembled my own, though she was not myself. There was total understanding and sympathy between us, as if she were my sister—though I have never had a sister. Her name, which she told me, was Hyphen. This vision returned to me in solitude over a long period. For several months I actually expected to meet her in the flesh, and I often had mental conversations with her. I sensed that she was for me both bride and sister, my complement, and I suppose that she could reasonably be regarded as being a vision of Anima by the Ego, of the buried feminine half of myself, as well as an erotic fantasy— though in fact she did not arouse me sexually as much as other dreams or fantasies. The name Hyphen was very clear. There was no mistaking it. Samuel Johnson described the Hyphen as 'a note of conjunctio' and derived it from the Greek. The face of this woman, this figure, still occasionally returns to me.

This vision is extraordinarily similar to the Muse figure described by many poets. I was not aware of this, however, at the time, except, per-haps, unconsciously, for by that time I had read most of the major English poets and was not totally ignorant of the more widely-known classical myths. This vision was one of kindness, of understanding, of absolute sympathy; it was, perhaps, Paradisal. Some time later, in 1945, a second vision occurred which was less comforting and more mysterious though equally potent. Again I was in a half waking condition, lying in a hospital bed in India. Quite suddenly, as if in the very hospital ward, there appeared before my inward eye the figure of a dark-haired and swarthy-skinned woman, full-breasted, red-lipped. I found myself both welcoming yet struggling against her presence, frightened of being in some way possessed, of being committed to something or someone too powerful for me to bear. As I struggled I attempted to hear the name which the vision embodied. 'Levaun' I heard, and felt myself unsure of its spelling, and then, more clearly, 'Drachmae, Drachmae Levaun'. I was certain of the spelling 'Drachmae' though I could not understand why the woman's given name should be that of a coin I associated vaguely with Latin texts. The word 'Levaun' I knew to be a foreign language. I wrote the names down and did not care to study them again for twenty-five years. Then, while puzzling over various aspects of Poetry and Poetic inspiration, I. decided to take the plunge and try to solve that ancient riddle. I assumed that the word 'Levaun' would be found in a French or German or Latin dictionary in some form or other as these were the three languages with which I had some skimpy knowledge in 1945. Eventually I found that Livourne was the French name for the Italian city, Livorno, which was known in English as Leghorn. Searching further I found that the Romans knew it as Libernum and Liberni Portus, this last name meaning 'Gate of the Ships'. The word Liberna means a two-masted ship known as a Brigantine or Hermaphrodite Brig, or any light swift craft used in the Mediterranean or the Levant, or a piratical vessel. The word 'Brigantine', however, if read in the context of a vision of a female and potently sexual figure, can only lead to the identification of Brigantia, the river-goddess of the Brigantes who once occupied the whole of Northern England from East to West, omitting only (oddly enough) the area of Holderness in which I was born, though my father and his ancestors were all born in Brigantes territory. The Brigantes, it appears, had several gods. One of them was a horned god, and here I remember Leghorn, and recall (what I did not know in 1945) that I had been born with my right leg broken at the thigh. Brigantia herself is identified both with the triple-goddess Brigid and with Minerva.

Here the interpretation takes another twist, for the Brigantine is also known as a Hermaphrodite Brig. The word Brig has as one meaning 'bridge'. Filey Brig, where I used to play as a boy, got its name from being regarded as a part-built bridge across the North Sea. Hermaphrodite was the child of Aphrodite (again) and Hermes. The winged sandals of Hermes may, Robert Graves suggests, indicate that he must keep his sacred heel lifted from the ground, and be a graphic indication that he has been ritually lamed in order to play king to the Muse Goddess. His role as a fertility god worshipped in the form of stone phalli sufficiently relates him to the word horn, which in my schooldays was a common word for an erection. According to Joseph Campbell,

> . . . a fundamental idea of *all* the pagan disciplines, both of the Orient and the Occident, during the period of which we are writing (first Millennium B.C.), was that the inward turning of the mind (symbolized by the sunset) should culminate in a realization *in esse* of the individual (microcosm) and the universe (macrocosm), which when achieved, would bring together in one order of act and realization the principles of eternity and time, sun and moon, male and female, Hermes and Aphrodite (Hermaphroditus) and the two serpents of the caduceus.[1]

It is at this point that it is worth considering the significance of the word 'Drachmae' for it appeared to me to be a qualifying word. The Greek Drachma was a silver coin, and the most famous version of it is the Athenian drachma, the design of which was also used by Alexander the Great. On the obverse of the coin is a head of Pallas Athene, and on the reverse an owl, a sprig of olive, and a crescent. Pallas Athene was, of course, the original of the Roman Minerva whom we have already identified with Brigantia. Moreover it is curious to note that Pallas Athene is reported as springing 'fully armed' from the head of Zeus and that the word Brigantine can also mean medieval coat of body armour.

Though to many readers this closely woven mesh of interpretations may seem little more than a farrago, it is unlikely to seem absurd to a poet, for the kind of symbolic connections by means of verbal echoes which I have adduced are precisely those which animate his imagination when writing poems. Moreover the poet is always able to be convinced of the truth of an experience when it can be shown to contain this tightly woven system of interpenetrating references. I can myself, however, no more summarize the precise meaning of my vision of Drachmae Levaun than I can summarize the experience of any true poem. I can only gloss it, as I might gloss a poem, with one or two tentative comments. I would suggest therefore that my vision was of the Muse as both

[1] Joseph Campbell, *The Masks of God: Occidental Mythology.* Viking/Compass 1970, pp. 163–164.

Wisdom (Minerva-Athena) and as Sexual Love (Hermes, Aphrodite, the lame God and the Horn); she showed herself open to receive and harbour (Portus) the offspring (Hermaphrodite) of Eloquence (Hermes) and Love (Aphrodite), and she established herself as the goddess of my ancestors (Brigantia) and offered wealth (Drachmae). My fear of her was caused by my recognition that I was being offered something that would possess me completely and alter my whole existence, and also, I suspect, by the darkness of her in contrast with the golden-haired Muse of my previous vision, and by the intensity of the sexual feeling her presence aroused. There was, I found myself saying afterwards, an element of paganism in the vision. I could fuse my vision of Hyphen into my inchoate Christian habit of mind, but I could not face Drachmae Levaun without abandoning many prejudices and inhibitions. I still am uncertain as to whether or not my caution was justified, and, in remembering that vision, I am still troubled for, though the surface of the riddle may now have been read, there were depths of experience quite untouched upon by the two words I was given to put aside for a quarter of a century.

THREE A Priestlike Task

I am not concerned in this book to explain (which so often means 'explain away') the kind of experiences presented in the last chapter. I wish simply to place them on record. Nevertheless anyone with a smattering of Jungian psychology will appreciate that the encounter with the Muse can be described in terms of the Ego confronting Anima, the 'feminine' and submerged half of the masculine psyche, which, when united with the Ego, in what Jung has called the *Conjunctio* (I think here, again, of my vision of Hyphen) leads to awareness of the total Self. If we do take a Jungian line it would seem logical to suppose that female poets perceive the Muse as male. This is frequently the case. Some, however, as Graves has suggested, feel themselves to be an embodiment of the Muse, or Her spokeswoman. Nevertheless they frequently make use of, or envision, a masculine figure as an important element in their poetic cosmogony. One young Canadian poetess was for a period unable to avoid writing of a black man, a clear vision of her Animus. Others have found themselves presented with visions of a man as a personification of both Love and Death, just as male poets have seen the Muse in these terms. The whole subject of the Muse is, however, complex, and it is unwise to summarize it thus briefly. In 1972 Kathleen Raine talked to me about the Muse–poet relationship. She said:

> There is no rule in the universe that the Muse is always feminine. It is feminine in relation to the masculine psyche. In my own case I have always—so far back as I can remember—been aware of an accompanying Daimon. I never called it the Muse, but I was always aware of it, or *him* as it was to me. I certainly thought of the Daimon as a youthful sort of Ariel figure, and my Daimon has come and gone according to whether I was on the beam of my poetry or not all through my life. And of course Plotinus doesn't speak of the Muse: he speaks of the Daimon, and Plato and the Neo-Platonists believed that everyone has their Daimon, the quality of the Daimon depending on the quality of the soul of the person in question. When the Delphic Oracle was consulted on Plotinus she said that his Daimon was the God himself. And this was very unusual because most people's Daimons are lower

down the scale of the celestial hierarchies. But Plato's teaching of the Daimon is very modern indeed, Jungian really. Whoever is born has an accompanying Daimon who is answerable for us to the Gods. This doctrine doesn't relate to the Animus-Anima; it relates to the Conscious–Unconscious because the Platonic Daimon would, from our point of view, correspond to the Unconscious which accompanies every conscious person throughout life and from time to time prompts and advises us for our good and to whom we may or may not listen. This is nearer to the Jungian idea of the Unconscious than the Freudian, certainly. The Daimon is thought, in the Platonic philosophy, always to be a source of greater wisdom and knowledge of a more divine order, and therefore is more in the nature of a Superconscious than a Subconscious. This I deeply believe to be true; whether it is regarded as masculine or feminine seems to me to be secondary, perhaps to depend on the sex of the person concerned. I told you long ago of my vision of the Sleeper Beneath the Tree who was a boy figure. I always feel that Ariel is very closely akin to my Daimon. So Shakespeare had the Ariel figure perhaps—the boy, the *puer eternus*—rather than the Anima. I don't think he was so much an Anima poet. I think his was the Daimon, the airy spirit. . . . Of course we do tend often to project these spiritual forms (upon people) but when one is writing poetry, in fact, one is consulting the Daimon, not any human person.

I suggested at this point that some masculine poets (and female poets too, for all that I knew), from time to time felt that the Muse was truly embodied in a specific person. I referred to Petrarch's *Sonnets to Laura,* and suggested that in that case there was a dialogue with the Muse in the form of a real person, though she was, in point of fact, either absent or dead for the greater part of the time. Kathleen Raine recalled the case of Dante and Beatrice and added 'I wonder if he would have written these things to Beatrice had she been living, because the dead inhabit the world of the invisible.' Our own dialogue continued:

I never confused the Daimon with the person I was in love with. That is something different. I have been deeply in love and much of my poetry arises from that, but I have never at any time confused the person I loved with the Daimon. The Daimon is something that exists entirely in one's own Psyche, or in relation to one's own Psyche. I would call it a Guardian Angel, perhaps, in Christian terms. But an accompanying spirit much more in the relation of Ariel with Prospero than of what one feels towards a person one loves. In Dante's case it seems that the two were, as you describe, fused in the figure of Beatrice, but then, remember, he set out with Virgil.

Who was a Daimon!

In part, certainly; also, in part, tradition, of course, but surely, as a dream-figure, more than that. Turning to the Daimon seems really what one does when one writes a poem. When one is in a good vein the approach sometimes comes from them. The invitation, as it were, comes in the form of some idea that is dropped in one's mind— something that darts into one's mind as if from without. It may be a line. It may be, as it were, the shape of a poem which hasn't yet got the words fitted to the shape. It may be a rhythm. It may be even something less tangible than that. But it is a living germ of a poem in some way.

Another, younger, woman poet, Susan Musgrave, talking of her experience of the Muse, said

I'm trying to remember what roles She plays in the poems and I think She's always trying to take me somewhere else. She's always moving; She's always leading away or towards . . . She's moving from the inside out, taking me with Her, like in that poem *Sounding*: 'She follows me attentive to the failing edge.' It's always that sort of thing; I'm Her at the same time but I'm the one that's being misled or deceived, and yet She's doing it. Maybe She's a part of me, not like a conscience, but some part of me that thinks I should be doing something else. But She's certainly separate because I do not think autobiographically at all about those sort of poems.

To the adolescent or young poet visions and obsessions of this kind can be deeply disturbing, as can other experiences which appear to be symptomatic of poethood, or at least to accompany it. Young adults, alone and idly thinking or dreaming, are often assailed by thoughts which appear to be expressed by another voice inside their heads. Sometimes these voices are so insistent as almost to seem physically audible. On occasion the young poet will experience apparent precognition, and instances of telepathic communication are frequent. Most of us have had some slight experiences of precognition and we usually dismiss them as lucky guesses or as coincidences. Most of us have experiences that could be labelled as telepathy; we choose however to dismiss them as relatively meaningless oddities. The poet, unable easily to dismiss anything which suggests that the imagination may have power, is inclined to take these matters more seriously, though not necessarily more earnestly. It is not possible to state whether poets are more frequently visited with extra-sensory perceptions than other folk, for no statistics are available. I would hazard the suspicion that extra-sensory perceptions are familiar to a large number of poets, however, and that these perceptions are often closely linked with their poetic activities. Susan Musgrave admits to many experiences of precognition. Sometimes, on meeting someone, she *knows* that they are nearing death, which disturbs her a great deal. She told me

> I have it in dreams a lot. I'll dream something is going to happen and it does the next day. A person will come. More than often it is a letter. I dream that I get a letter from someone and when I wake up it's there.

Sometimes poems themselves appear to contain pre-cognitive elements. This happened to me with my own poem, *Toad*. The poem runs:

> The crack in the rock split wide to our drill;
> in a hollow round as a skull
> was a still toad, held in unbreathing,
> as if this cell
> were sanctuary in the perpetual rock of grieving.
>
> and we held back as dust on the blurred skin
> spread its grey stain,
> thinking the rock trapped him in his rainy leaping
> to make this prison,
> and held our hands to what was smally heaving
>
> as if with the sudden sun-slap some living will
> has been brightly spilled
> into the stiff bulk, watched the blink and the fumbling
> limbs that were limbs still
> hop over the stone chips, roused to sky and stumbling.
>
> and said, 'When small he was held by the hollow stone,
> but, tranced, lived on:
> life locked from the start in its one little room
> can still burn song,
> hidden, have flame till what drill split the tomb ?'[1]

Some months after this poem had been published, I read of an archeologist in Greece having the experience I described. The report was in *The Sunday Times*. Another instance is of my poem *Ballad of Despair* which describes how a man, tormented by the thought of a possible atomic holocaust, first killed his wife and children and then himself. Once

---

[1] Robin Skelton, *Selected Poems 1947–1967*. McClelland and Stewart 1968, p. 18.

again, some time after the poem had been completed, a man in Glasgow acted in exactly the way that the poem described. Instances of precognition in poetry are not infrequent, but poets tend to avoid discussion of them. There is an uneasy, irrational, but deep-seated feeling that the poem may somehow not have foreseen, but have *caused* the events it described. Poets, like small children and magicians, cannot help believing that words may affect reality. The words have been given 'power' by the intensity with which they have been 'spoken', by the special form and voice that has been used. Many poets are in the habit of invoking the Muse before tackling a difficult work, as Milton does at the commencement of *Paradise Lost*. A larger number of poets than one might suppose use their poetic abilities to write spells of healing. A few, a very few, write curses. J. M. Synge once wrote a curse on 'a sister of an enemy of the author's who disapproved of *The Playboy*'

> The Curse
> Lord, confound this surly sister,
> Blight her brow with blotch and blister,
> Cramp her larynx, lung, and liver,
> In her guts a galling give her.
> Let her live to earn her dinners
> In Mountjoy with seedy sinners:
> Lord, this judgment quickly bring,
> And I'm your servant, J. M. Synge.[1]

According to W. B. Yeats the curse had some effect: Yeats reported in his Journal 'when he showed me this, he said with mirthful eyes that since he had written it, her husband had got drunk, gone with a harlot, got syphilis, and given it to his wife.'[2]

Robert Graves has told us how the Ollamhs of Ancient Ireland could raise blotches on the skins of their enemies by means of their satirical verse. Some poets have found themselves attempting straightforward healing spells. One poet I know, who wishes to remain anonymous, claims a seventy-five per cent success in his spells of healing. In one instance he wrote a spell to cure a verruca of two years standing, one that had made the sufferer unable to walk. Surgery was planned. The verruca disappeared, leaving no scar tissue. The surgeon credited the patient's 'witch' with the cure.

[1] Robin Skelton (ed.), *J. M. Synge, Collected Works. Vol I: Poems*. Oxford University Press 1962, p. 49.
[2] Denis Donoghue (ed.), *W. B. Yeats: Memoirs*. The Macmillan Company 1972, p. 202.

I have reports of other cures by poets, including cases of arthritis, anal bleeding, laryngitis, and even Hodgkins Disease.

Whether or not we accept all these 'cures' as having been caused by poetic acts, we must, I think, record that many poets do believe in the power of verbal magic. Susan Musgrave told me of one spell she wrote.

> It was really a powerful one and it started to work, and I got kind of anxious towards the end and stopped doing it. . . . It was really working, which was frightening. I wrote one to turn someone mad but I never used it because I decided it would be pretty dangerous.

Many of today's young believe firmly in magic, and in the efficacy of charms and spells. Kathleen Raine told me that she too believes in magic, and said

> I have felt, actually, that I *am* the Lady Rokujo from Murasaki. The No Drama takes perfect cognizance of the fact that people's thoughts take effect, whether in the form of a curse or a prayer, and if we believe in prayer we must also believe in cursing. In fact prayer is magic, isn't it ? Thoughts transmit themselves, and a powerful thought will always transmit itself whether for good or evil. We are protected, mercifully on the whole, from the knowledge of the power of our thoughts. That is one reason why I never put my darkest thoughts into poetry. I never, I think, have written a poem unless I hoped to make it in some sense a positive statement because all art has that magical quality and by putting the nihilistic or otherwise what one calls evil into form one is setting it loose in the world, and it will take effect, and I would scruple to do this. . . . I think Art can be put into the service of evil forces. We at our peril disbelieve in evil.

She went on to suggest that one of the functions of poetry might well be magical, and that perhaps one might consider the making of healing and protective spells as a proper part of the poet's role. Poets, do, in fact, from time to time deliberately attempt magical acts as distinct from using magical structures or allusions in their poems. One instance of this I find particularly interesting. It occurred a year or two ago. An author of considerable experience was suffering from acute financial embarrassment; the cause of it was a publisher on the other side of the world. The writer's very living was endangered. Seated in a café in Europe, drinking wine, with three poets, all well known and one famous, he complained of his predicament. The elder of the three poets said matter-of-factly, 'Well, we ought to be able to do something about that' and the two other poets agreed. The three poets then concentrated upon the matter, in silence, for a period of perhaps a minute and then the eldest poet said, 'Well, that's done!' The two other poets agreed, absolutely certain that the problem had been solved. Some weeks later the man's difficulties were resolved, largely, it seems, by a total volte-face on the part of the publisher.

What is, I think, interesting about this story is the calm and matter-of-fact way in which the three poets, who knew each other only very slightly and one of whom had never met the eldest poet before that afternoon, were able to join together in an action that to most people would seem ridiculous.

All this may seem to have little to do with the actual writing of poetry. It does, however, illustrate the degree to which the poet believes in the significance of language and the power of the imagination, and indicates that, while not all poets make spells, all poets treat the act of writing and the act of speech as being significant and effective in a fashion quite different from that in which they are regarded as significant and effective by propagandists, journalists, and (I regret to say) the vast majority of academics. It also points to the way in which dedicated poets, as distinct from occasional poem-makers, find themselves relating to their experiences and intuitions in a way that appears to be quite different from that of the majority. They not only 'see through' experience to another and (some would say) eternal world; they also feel that speech and thought have powers that demand perpetual vigilance and reverence in their use. Those poets who express this aspect of their attitudes and beliefs most explicitly are usually labelled by critics as 'mystics' and thus set apart from 'Ordinary' poets. We have had the label 'mystical' attached to those poems of Wordsworth, Coleridge, Shelley, Byron, Keats, and the later Romantics which present the nature of the poetic experience most clearly. We have seen Blake and Christopher Smart labelled as 'mystics' and as 'madmen'; we have seen Yeats' discussions of the poetic character described as 'mumbo jumbo'. Indeed, all too often, there has been an attempt to regard those poets, whose explorations of the numinous, the eternal, and the magical are entirely typical of dedicated poets everywhere, as exceptions to an as yet undetermined rule. Even Walter Sutton, writing sympathetically of Emerson's view of poetry, uses the words 'Transcendentalist' and 'mystical' in such a way as to suggest that Emerson's view is exceptional and (by using the phrase 'was to Emerson' at one point) idiosyncratic. His summary is, however, useful. It runs:

In *Nature* (1836), Emerson first formulated the Transcendentalist theory that he was to elaborate in essays published over the following twenty or thirty years, but without any significant change in outlook. In all his writing Emerson celebrated the imagination as a power of mystical perception. In 'The Poet', the imagination is described as 'a very high sort of seeing, which does not come by study, but by the intellect being where and what it sees.' Through this power, which resolves the subject-object dichotomy and man's alienation from the world of natural objects, the poet was to Emerson an 'integrating seer', even a 'liberating God' who could show man the divine fact amid appearances. The highest function of poetry was, accordingly, to provide a transcendental stairway to the stars of divine truth.[1]

Emerson held this view all his life, and it is a view which poets have held from the earliest times to the present.

This view of the poet as an 'integrating seer' and 'liberating God' runs counter to the view, held by some, that a poet's work is always highly personal, and that, indeed, it is possible to relate a man's poems quite sensibly and directly to his psychological condition. Thus, during the past decade, there has been a proliferation of psycho-analytical criticism (particularly from Freudians) and the poet has become for many eager academic careerists a kind of laboratory specimen, or perhaps the most ideal patient, forever prone upon the couch and forever uncovering his neuroses and traumas.

It would be stupid to pretend that poets do not have neuroses, and that their psychological condition does not enter into and sometimes even animate their poems. Poets naturally explore those experiences and memories to which life (and perhaps inheritance) has made them most sensitive, and they use, in their explorations, those images which appear to them to be most potent. Nevertheless, this psycho-analytical approach remains little more than a sophisticated version of the old notion that a poem is always a piece of thinly disguised autobiography, and that the poet (unlike the novelist) cannot ever really step sufficiently outside or beyond his own experience to imagine feelings he has not himself suffered or experiences he has not himself known. One of the difficulties the poet faces in explaining his way of life to others is, in fact, the near impossibility of ever describing the way in which his poetry relates at once to personal experience and to supra-personal visions and intuitions. Sometimes the average reader may be correct in assuming that a poem written

[1] Walter Sutton, *American Free Verse, the Modern Revolution in Poetry*. New Directions 1973, p. 6.

in the first person is a record of actual experience or the expression of emotions which the poet has felt deeply enough for him to be compelled to put them down on paper. Some poems are clearly of this kind, but many are not the records of previously experienced thoughts or feelings but themselves the occasions of those thoughts and feelings. The cry of pain or of delight may be the discovery of the poem itself; the poem may bring to the writer the experience and the emotion which is its subject. Even the poem based firmly upon actual experience is rarely factually true. It either distorts facts or combines them in such a way as to recreate the original event in a fashion that makes the whole completely unreliable as documentation of actuality. 'Poets should be good liars' said Yeats, and he meant that the poet must transform the actual in such a way as to permit it to reveal truths and perceptions which the accurate recording of actuality would not permit. Wordsworth, in writing what appear to be autobiographical poems, habitually combined events which had occurred at different points in time and space so as to enable the poem to present its vision the more effectively. It was emotional, not factual, truth that he was concerned to present. Sometimes these manœuvres completely disguise the original experience. I recall, myself, that in writing one particular love poem which was an attempt to explore the nature of that mutual dependence upon deceit which can act both as a bond between lovers and as the cause of eventual disruption of the relationship, I 'constructed' the girl in the scenario from several observations and experiences spanning thirty years. The scene I envisaged was a cliff that I knew as a small boy. The girl, for symbolic reasons, had red-bronze hair and brown eyes, but was not any girl I have ever known. The whole 'experience' of the poem, as regards fact, was invented; the emotions expressed were not entirely invented, but rather exaggerated versions of remembered qualms. The whole poem, written in the first person, however, sounds like a record of actual experience.

In this way the poet is, perhaps, operating in the same way as the novelist or the playwright. Unlike the majority of novelists and playwrights, however, he reorganizes his experience not only in order to present a semblance of actual human experience, but also in order to imply some metaphysical truth. He maximizes emotions not to display those emotions for their own sake but in order to present something additional. In an earlier book about poetry I described this process as it occurred in the making of a particular poem of mine, *The Ball*.

I was in Cornwall, on a long holiday, and a friend took me along to a rocky promontory that juts out into the Atlantic called Carn Vellan.

Being a painter, he was fascinated by colours, and he told me that in a cavern that had been made by a huge slab of rock roofing in a narrow inlet, there was one of those hollow iron floats that fishermen use. It had been rolled up the narrow cavern by the tide, and been jammed in the crevice where the roof, floor, and walls met. It was thus fixed at the very top of a hollow cone of rock. The wind and weather had coloured this ball in a dramatic manner. It was, he said, orange and red and ochre, and extremely attractive. He wanted to see if we could get it out of the cavern and take it home.

The only way into the cavern was by squeezing ourselves through a gap in the roof, which was level with the ground on which we stood, and lowering ourselves down to the floor, about ten feet below. He gave me his hand and I slithered into the cave, just managing to avoid a big pool directly below me. The sea, which blocked the entrance to the cave, boomed and roared. I was convinced that the tide was coming in. I could see the ball stuck fast about twenty-five feet away and I crawled towards it, but the cavern became so narrow that I could not get near. I poked at it with a stick, but it was no use, and I almost got stuck in my attempts to slither nearer.

As I was hauled out of the cave, a bit bruised and not a little shaken by the claustrophobic atmosphere I had experienced, I felt that, some-how, this adventure was significant. I said to myself, 'There's a poem here somewhere', but it was three or four weeks later that, idly wandering about my flat, a line came into my head, and I knew that the poem was ready to be written. I wrote it almost exactly as you read it now. It needed no altering to speak of; I made only a very few minor adjustments.

> Under the rock is an iron ball.
> If you lie on your belly you'll see it there,
> jammed between rock and rock at the top
> of the roofed-in creek, so changed by air
> and sea and age that its orange rust
> burns like a sun. It is held fast where
> rock meets rock. If you slither down
> on a rope, he said, you can get quite near.
>
> If you once get down, avoiding the pool
> that is three foot deep, worn round by a stone
> turning and turning upon the spool
> of the spinning tide, and are big enough fool
> to wedge your shoulders into that gap
> you can touch the ball. It is rough with rust
> and orange and ochre and red, he said,
> a sun clamped down by a granite crust,

but you'll never move it. The sea is loud
as your heart as you lie on the slime and shift
your hand past your head as you chin the stone,
and every time that you try to lift
a muscle or twist the tide seems near
and the rock roof closer. The ball burns red
where roof meets rock. I hid it there
when I was a child of God, he said.

It is easy to see just how the facts had been altered by my three or four
weeks of subconscious consideration of the experience. Most obvious is
the way in which the whole picture has been made more dramatic by
exaggerating the danger and difficulty of the exploit. The rope suggests
the cavern was deeper than it in fact was. The actual touching of the
ball makes the failure to move it appear even more frustrating. The
repetition of words like *rock* and *ball*, and the continual mention of the
threatening tide, gives the story an obsessive quality. Moreover, much
to my surprise when I wrote the poem, the story has become one told
by someone else, by an unidentified and therefore mysterious, stranger.
There is no explanation of why the stranger wanted to get the ball.
Had I said he was a painter, it would have removed the mystery. The
last line, which ties up the whole poem, and suggests that the story is
some kind of parable, came to me as a complete shock. I did not, at
first, know what on earth it meant. Then I began to see what had
happened. I had quite unconsciously realized that the descent into
darkness to try to reach the ball reflected man's continual attempts to
reach out for an ideal. The object being a ball, and compared to the
sun, made the adventure seem like that of a man seeking to capture
something immensely vital, almost a world, or a planet. The last line
suggested that the stranger had been seeking for a world of innocence,
or of purity, which he had deliberately and mistakenly put aside for
other things as he grew older. Now he wishes to return to the youthful
innocence, the vitality, he has lost. Thus the poem became, not
through any conscious intention on my part, a statement of a universal
human predicament.

The subconscious process that led to all these alterations can be
guessed at, if we simply think of the ideas that come to us when we
think of exploring caves for treasure. We have Aladdin's cave in mind
almost immediately. We may think of Grendel's cave in the story of
Beowulf. Psychologists have told us that man's fascination with caves
may be due to a deep-seated wish to return to the womb, and this
would be a not inappropriate idea to have in mind while reading this
poem, because of the reference to childhood with which it concludes.
Thus the subconscious process seems to have been that of selecting,

from all the available data, those details which carry the richest associations.

On the other hand, there are purely private reasons why I should have been led to make this poem. As a boy I lived by the sea, and spent a good deal of my time on the beach. Some of my earliest memories are of the seashore. Moreover, my grandmother lived at Filey in those days, and, as a very small boy, I would spend some part of the summer there, and I grew fascinated by the rocks and seaweed and caves and pools of Filey Brig, where my father would take me on mackerel-fishing trips. Thus, there is a purely personal reason why I should associate sea-caves with childhood. It is noticeable, however, that my subconscious, while recognizing this link, was clever enough not to assume, simply because rocks and seaweed and fishermen's iron floats (I played with many of them on the Yorkshire coast as a boy) brought thoughts of childhood to me, that they would bring childhood ideas to anyone else. Consequently the cave is given the qualities of a fairy-tale cave, and childhood is mentioned explicitly at the end of the poem.[1]

In *The Ball* I made use of childhood memories while writing about an adult experience. The poet is usually much more 'in contact' with his childhood than other folk, or at least more aware of that contact. He values some experiences because they connect his childhood fears and delights with his adult life and thus enable him, perhaps only momentarily, to feel that his life has a pattern and a unity. Many poets continually dwell upon childhood experiences, or utilize images from their childhood. Poets are absolutely unable to 'put away childish things'. In his *Autobiography* Edwin Muir describes how a particular event of his own childhood reappeared, transformed, in a poem written in middle age.

The day I remember best was the day when Freddie Sinclair chased me home: it was after we had gone to Helye, and his road lay in the same direction as mine. He was the boy I had fought over the knife, and this day he wanted to fight me again, but I was afraid. The road from the school to Helye lay on the crown of the island, and as I ran on, hollow with fear, there seemed to be nothing on either side of me but the sky. What I was so afraid of I did not know; it was not Freddie, but something else; yet I could no more have turned and faced him than I could have stopped the sun revolving. As I ran I was conscious only of a few huge things, monstrously simplified and enlarged: Wyre, which I felt under my feet, the other islands lying round, the sun in the sky, and the sky itself, which was quite empty. For almost thirty years

[1] Robin Skelton, *Poetry* (in the *Teach Yourself Books* series). English Universities Press 1963, pp. 19–23.

afterwards I was so ashamed of that moment of panic that I did not dare to speak of it to anyone, and drove it out of my mind. I was seven at the time, and in the middle of my guilty fears. On that summer afternoon they took the shape of Freddie Sinclair, and turned him into a terrifying figure of vengeance. I felt that all the people of Wyre, as they worked in their fields, had stopped and were watching me, and this tempered my fear with some human shame. I hoped that none of my family had noticed me, but when they came in from the fields at tea-time Sutherland said, 'Weel, boy, I see thu can run!' I had got over my panic by then, and pretended that Freddie and I had been having a race. Sutherland laughed. 'Ay, a fine race, man, a fine race!' He called me 'man' when he wanted to be sarcastic.

I got rid of that terror almost thirty years later in a poem describing Achilles chasing Hector round Troy, in which I pictured Hector returning after his death to run the deadly race over again. In the poem I imagined Hector as noticing with intense, dreamlike precision certain little things, not the huge simplified things which my conscious memory tells me I noticed in my own flight. The story is put in Hector's mouth:

> The grasses puff a little dust
> Where my footsteps fall,
> I cast a shadow as I pass
> The little wayside wall.
>
> The strip of grass on either hand
> Sparkles in the light,
> I only see that little space
> To the left and to the right,
>
> And in that space our shadows run,
> His shadow there and mine,
> The little knolls, the tossing weeds,
> The grasses frail and fine.

That is how the image came to me, quite spontaneously: I wrote the poem down, almost complete, at one sitting. But I have wondered since whether that intense concentration on little things, seen for a moment as the fugitive fled past them, may not be a deeper memory of that day preserved in a part of my mind which I cannot tap for ordinary purposes. In any case the poem cleared my conscience. I saw that my shame was a fantastically elongated shadow of a childish moment, imperfectly remembered; an untapped part of my mind supplied what my conscious recollection left out, and I could at last see the incident whole by seeing it as happening, on a great and tragic scale, to someone else. After I had written the poem the flight itself was changed, and with that my feelings towards it.[1]

From these two instances we can see that the poet is concerned, consciously or unconsciously, not simply to record, but to transmute experience. He looks at experience as something that can be changed. As a consequence he tends to approach even the ordinary and commonplace events of the day in the fashion of a sculptor surveying a piece of stone and wondering whether or not there is something that can be done with it. He looks for the shape hidden in the stone and tries to see how it can be released. Poets, as a consequence, often appear to be a little detached from events. They are watchful even when they appear most relaxed, and yet their watchfulness is not that of the average novelist. They are less concerned to observe details of appearance, or to note down particularities than they are to select, often intuitively, material capable of transformation. This is achieved less by intellectual concentration than by a kind of relaxed receptivity, which can look almost like sleep-walking. The poet who senses that there is 'something there', that there is something usable in a particular place or occasion, will appear to withdraw into himself, and even will often walk apart in order to avoid being disturbed while he is gathering his material, allowing impressions to flow into him. Commenting upon Wordsworth's schoolboy poem *Idyllium*, Mary Moorman wrote:

> In the last lines, however, he reveals the presence in his mind of a faculty or power of perceiving images, and also the joy which that creative power gave him. Nowhere else in his poetry does he describe so clearly this most significant mental process; the little poem is therefore important for the glimpse it gives us of his interior life; the development of a growing power of vision which became the foundation of all that was greatest in his poetry. After reproaching the 'nymphs' for allowing the death of the dog, he thus recalls how on their walks together:

> > If, while I gazed to Nature blind,
> > In the calm Ocean of my mind
> > Some new-created image rose
> > In full-grown beauty at its birth,
> > Lovely as Venus from the sea
> > Then, while my glad hand sprung to thee,
> > We were the happiest pair on earth.

[1] Edwin Muir, *An Autobiography*. Hogarth Press 1954, pp. 42–43.

The phrase 'while I gazed to Nature blind' has special significance, for it shows that he was now doing what became habitual with him— looking through or beyond the outward images that were the raw material of his vision into the mysterious depths of his own creative imagination, which was 'a calm Ocean', a receptive mirror in which he could perceive, with the clarity of a landscape emerging from a mist—the poetic image which had been eluding his intellectual search. It was the experience familiar to him from early childhood of the visionary capacity of his mind in certain circumstances, when everything seemed interior to his own being, and

> all I saw
> Appeared like something in myself, a dream,
> A prospect in the mind,

but now it was kindling to creative life. It is perhaps in this early fragment that he comes nearest to showing us the link between the passive and the active, the receptive and the creative states of his inner life.[1]

As I have already pointed out, the case of Wordsworth has been regarded as exceptional. Because he has recorded more exactly than any other poet the trance-like nature of his process of perception he has been called a 'mystic'. I must, however, repeat that Wordsworth's experience is not particularly rare among poets; it is, indeed, something of a commonplace of the poetic experience.

We must not, however, run away with the notion that this 'passive receptivity', this 'wise passiveness' or 'negative capability' is only brought into play when the poet is wandering around the countryside or contemplating particular places. It occurs, perhaps, even more frequently in the study. The poet utilizes his ability to dwell upon matters with a receptive passivity when he is engaged upon reading the works of others. A line or verse, an anecdote in a biography, even a phrase, can send him the signal 'this is usable—this can be transformed'. I myself 'found' two poems in Darwin's *Journal of the Beagle*, for example, and made poems from prose anecdotes. Other poets have chosen to use poems in a similar fashion. Robert Lowell's *Imitations of Sappho* are not translations but, he tells us, 'really new poems based on hers'. In 'imitating' Rilke's *Roman Sarcophagus* he added two new stanzas. He was, he says, 'reckless with literary meaning'. In this he resembles Ezra Pound in his 'translations' or, rather, recreations of Sextus Propertius and the Con-

[1] Mary Moorman, *William Wordsworth, A Biography*. Oxford University Press 1957, Vol I, p. 66.

fucian Odes. Samuel Johnson treated Juvenal in a similarly cavalier fashion, and many seventeenth-century poets produced 'Biblical paraphrases' which are really poetic expansions of and comments upon biblical stories.

Discussion of this kind of 'theft', or even (one might call it) plagiarism may seem to have led us away from the presentation of the state of 'passive receptivity'; it has, however, emphasized the essential characteristic of the poet's attitude towards all experience, whether physical or intellectual. The poet's cry is 'Transform!'

Behind this compulsion to change lies a belief, sometimes consciously held as such, and sometimes merely accepted as an attitude; this is that the outward forms of this world, the rocks, the trees, the people, the events, and even the world's existing literature and art, are messages which tell, when properly interpreted, of another kind of reality. The poet's task is to relate everything to that other reality, to challenge all surfaces and appearances, to make new patterns from old, and to do so, not by conscious ingenuity alone, but by utilizing the sensitivities and organizational powers of the subconscious, and thus bringing to bear upon experience not a part but the whole of the human armoury of perceptiveness. Wordsworth saw the poet's as a 'priest-like task', and while a good many living poets would boggle at the 'holier than thou' implications of the phrase, most of them would agree that the poetic and religious vocations have much in common.

FOUR Poet's Workshop

Poetry is an 'art' and a 'mystery', but it is also a craft. I have already quoted Goethe's words, 'The artist who is not also a craftsman is no good'. When poets meet to look over each other's work the discussion is very rarely of themes and meanings, but most usually of technique. Words are attacked for being imprecise; lines are queried in terms of their cadence or their speed; devices of assonance, consonance, and alliteration are scrutinized. Though the language used is almost never that of the semanticist, grammarian, or scholar of rhetoric, the analyses are frequently much more subtle and thorough than those of accredited scholars. Poets do, indeed, tend to find the analyses of professional critics and scholars who are not themselves poetic craftsmen both clumsy and boring, and concerned usually with inessentials. Here again the poet finds himself at odds with society, and especially with the usual academic approaches to literature. Matters which he regards as of supreme importance are ignored by most critics, and matters which he considers of marginal significance are treated as central. Thus, in lectures on Hardy, it is common to have long disquisitions upon Hardy's attitudes, beliefs, and images, but very little reference to his extraordinary handling of metre, of unequal lines, and of a mixed diction. Lecturers on Yeats rarely comment upon his development of a highly idiosyncratic syntax. Critics of Dylan Thomas avoid commenting more than superficially and evasively upon the structure of his poems. Poetry is treated all too often as if it were fiction, drama, autobiography, or philosophy, and the craftsmanship is ignored. This has become so general a situation in the educational system in the English speaking world that young would-be poets are inclined to suspect all talk of prosody as mere pedantry, and 'honours' students of English cannot tell an anapaest from a dactyl.

The poet's life is complicated by this general ignorance of the technicalities of his work. He knows that he must study his craft, but he can find few aids to this study. Most works on prosody are unhelpful. They may explain the basic formula of, let us say, dactyllic hexameter; they do not explain anything more. It is as if an apprentice cabinet maker were to be told how to recognize cedar, or mahogany, or spruce, but not told anything about the hardness, the grain, or the other characteristics of any of them. It is as if a music student were to be told how to recognize a violin, but not how to play it.

Poets in search of that kind of instruction in the craft which they need are usually obliged either to resign themselves to working by trial and error or to seek out those few books in which poets comment upon the structure of verse. In doing this they will often find themselves in disagreement with accepted opinion. Robert Graves, for example, in the teeth of scores of critics who have praised the verse of Alexander Pope, has commented:

> If I had time, I should be charmed to take you line by line through any long poem of Pope's you pleased, demonstrating its technical incompetency when judged by the standards of his predecessors and successors. Pope has no control of his *s's*, he does not sufficiently vary his vowel sounds, his antitheses are forced, his poetic vocabulary inexact, his inversions of syntax are not only un-English but misleading. As a test of my opinion, while preparing this lecture, I opened *Pope's Works* at random, and came across this six-line passage from his *Imitations of Horace*. It should have been carried through three more drafts at least.

> > Let Envy howl, while Heaven's whole chorus sings,
> > And bark at honour not conferred by Kings . . .

> *Envy* and *Heaven*, like *howl*, *while*, and *whole*, are too close in sound to occur decently in the same line, *Howl*, *Heaven*, and *whole* are over-alliterative. *Chorus sings* is not as tuneful as the sense requires. The suggested antithesis between the Heavenly Chorus and royal honours can hardly be intended.

> > Let Flattery sickening see the incense rise
> > Sweet to the world and grateful to the skies . . .

> Pope's *s's* are quite out of hand here. And does he mean that Flattery sickens others, or that Flattery itself falls sick ? And if the latter, was this sickness antecedent to the right of rising incense, or due to it ?

> Do *the skies* mean merely the sky, to which the fumes ascend, as opposed to the earth; or do they mean God's Heaven, as opposed to this world of men ? And is the incense a flattering incense, or is it an incense which all devout Catholics, like Pope, are required to burn ?

> > Truth guards the poet, sanctifies the line
> > And makes immortal, verse so mean as mine.

> *The* incense, *the* world, *the* skies, *the* poet, *the* line ! Five *the's* in nineteen

words. Pope could never control his definite article. And does *the line* stand for the lines of a poet's verse, or the line of succession—as he uses it three couplets later. *-fies the line* is ugly. *Makes immortal, verse so mean as mine* is over-alliterative again, and the inversion of 'makes verse so mean as mine immortal' calls for an awkward comma to separate *immortal* from *verse*—otherwise the sense would be:

'And makes even immortal verse as mean as mine'.

The Dunciad (its revision provoked by a fancied slight from Cibber in the matter of a stage-crocodile) was supposedly aimed at dullness. But is anything duller in the world than the ideal of correctness, even if not seriously framed ?[1]

Robert Graves' criticism has aroused a great deal of anger for he has chosen to comment unfavourably upon the craftsmanship of a large number of revered poets, both dead and living. He is, however, the only poet-critic I know who constantly reveals on the page that concern for structure which the poet himself must have if he is to perfect his verse. Graves' criticism leads him frequently to rewrite, or revise, those poems he finds flawed. This, again, strikes many as an impertinence. It would not have struck the authors of the Greek Anthology so; they frequently revised and rewrote epigrams by their predecessors. Rochester thought it no sin to rewrite Quarles, nor Dryden, Chaucer. To the poet literature is not a museum whose objects must be untouched by human hand. In reading any poem that seems flawed to him the poet will, quite automatically, consider possible revisions, even though he may not write them down. I myself have been irritated for thirty-five years by a poem Leigh Hunt wrote which I cannot help delighting in as a gay, neatly made poem, even though one line is, to me absolutely unacceptable. The poem is his famous *Rondeau*

> Jenny kissed me when we met,
>   Jumping from the chair she sat in;
> Time, you thief, who love to get
>   Sweets into your list, put that in!
> Say I'm weary, say I'm sad,
>   Say that health and wealth have missed me,
> Say I'm growing old, but add
>   Jenny kiss'd me.

I cannot understand why a thief should busy himself making lists; nor does it seem likely that a thief would make a list of 'sweets' of any kind.

[1] Robert Graves, *The Crowning Privilege*. Cassell 1955, pp. 34–36.

Moreover, I do not understand why Time, that thief, should record the poet's state of health as if he were some kind of doctor on a daily visit. Possibly the thief Time should be transformed into the Recording Angel, whose duty it is to detail the lives of men ? Then we could have 'Gabriel, who loves to get. . . .' But the hard 'g's' are not euphonious, and sound harsh. Perhaps it could be 'Recording Angel, keen to get. . . .' but again the hard 'c's' intrude upon the lightness of the poem. The word *sweets* still demands attention also. Perhaps we could have:

> Scribbling Angel, if you set
> Down any miracle, put that in ?

But in what ? In his list or record. Then:

> Scribbling Angel, if you set
> Down triumphs in your list, put that in.

Or, more colloquially,

> Scribbling Angel, if you're set
> On listing miracles, get that in!

miracles seems wrong, however. It suggests that the poet prizes the oddity of the occasion rather than its sweetness. Would *ecstasies* do ? There would be rather too many 's' sounds. The poem would splutter instead of sing.

> Scribbling Angel, do not let
> the page be blotted without that in!

Now the line begins with an unstressed instead of a stressed syllable. Perhaps it could be:

> Scribbling Angel, do not let
> Life record me without that in.

One could go on almost forever.

   This, certainly, is the feeling that most poets have when working on a poem, whether it is one of their own, or another's. Although, ideally, the finished poem is unalterable in all respects, down to the least mark of punctuation, the cadence of the most unimportant syllable, few poets are ever totally convinced that any of their poems cannot be improved. As Robert Graves said once, 'No poem is ever perfected'. Bearing all this in mind, it is, perhaps, natural that when poets are asked which of their poems they like the best they often pick one of whose craftsmanship they are proud, and in commenting upon the poem show their delight in the skill (which they have laboured to possess) rather than in the vision or perception for which they feel less personally responsible. Thus in

Joseph Langland's fascinating Anthology *Poets Choice*, in which poets selected favourites among their own poems, several of the contributors admitted that they chose the poem for largely technical reasons. Robert Francis, for example, presented the following poem and comment:

Hallelujah: A Sestina

A wind's word, the Hebrew Hallelujah.
I wonder they never give it to a boy
(Hal for short) boy with wind-wild hair.
It means Praise God, as well it should since praise
Is what God's for. Why didn't they call my father
Hallelujah instead of Ebenezer?

Eben, of course, but christened Ebenezer,
Product of Nova Scotia (hallelujah).
Daniel, a country doctor, was his father
And my father his tenth and final boy.
A baby and last, he had a baby's praise:
Red petticoat, red cheeks, and crow-black hair.

A boy has little say about his hair
And little about a name like Ebenezer
Except that he can shorten either. Praise
God for that, for that shout Hallelujah.
Shout Hallelujah for everything a boy
Can be that is not his father or grandfather.

But then, before you know it, he is a father
Too and passing on his brand of hair
To one more perfectly defenseless boy,
Dubbing him John or James or Ebenezer
But never, so far as I know, Hallelujah,
As if God didn't need quite that much praise.

But what I'm coming to—Could I ever praise
My father half enough for being a father
Who let me be myself? Sing Hallelujah.
Preacher he was with a prophet's head of hair
And what but a prophet's name was Ebenezer,
However little I guessed it as a boy?

Outlandish names of course are never a boy's
Choice. And it takes time to learn to praise.
Stone of Help is the meaning of Ebenezer.
Stone of Help—what fitter name for my father?
Always the Stone of Help however his hair
Might graduate from black to Hallelujah.

> Such is the old drama of boy and father.
> Praise from a grayhead now with thinning hair.
> Sing Ebenezer, Robert, sing Hallelujah!

If you drape thirty-nine iron chains over your arms and shoulders and then do a dance, the whole point of the dance will be to seem light and effortless. Commenting on *Hallelujah: A Sestina*, several people said: 'We don't know what a sestina is but we enjoy the poem. It made your father vivid.' I was both irked and pleased.

It was the first sestina I ever attempted. What made it a little easier was an idea I had before I started. If six words are to be repeated over and over, two things should be true of them: (1) they should be words so 'useful' that the ear will keep track of all their recurrences and (2) enjoy the pattern of chiming. Such a word, for instance, as *hallelujah*. That word suggested another Hebrew one, *Ebenezer*. With these two words as a starter, I was on my way. Out of these two words grew everything I found to say.

Yet in starting to write a sestina I was really going against my deepest poetic convictions. For a sestina is an extreme example of a poem written from the outside in, and my way is to write from the inside out. To encourage a poem, as it grows, to grow its own skeleton and skin. Like a living cat. And not to start with the skin, as the taxidermist does, and stuff it out. I am strong for form, but not for forms. Perhaps I should now admit that a poem written the wrong way may sometimes be more successful than a poem written the right way.

I have no favourite poem or poems. Enough to say that this poem is one of peculiar interest to me.

ROBERT FRANCIS[1]

The comments of the other poets are also indicative of this interest in the craft of verse. John Crowe Ransom said of *Prelude to an Evening* 'The four-beat lines don't count the syllables, nor make rhymes, and that being exceptional pleased the poet.'[2] Allen Tate said of his *The Mediterranean*, 'The poem is obviously in iambic pentameter, but I made a point of not writing any two lines in the same rhythm'.[3] Phyllis McGinley said, with reference to her *Ballade of Lost Objects*, 'I love verse-skills and feel I have demonstrated here that ornamental forms can carry a certain weight of

---

[1] Joseph Langland (ed.), *Poets Choice*. Dial Press 1962, pp. 46–47.
[2] ibid., p. 12.
[3] ibid., p. 40.

thought and poignancy'.[1] Theodore Roethke said of *Words for the Wind*, 'The piece is written in a line-length that interested me from the beginning'.[2] Robert Graves, writing of *A Troll's Nosegay* said, 'The technical problem was how to make a sonnet read as though it were not a sonnet, while keeping the rules'.[3] It is almost impossible to disentangle the poet's exploration of a theme from his struggle to achieve perfect form, since to him the theme and the form are fused together in the one endeavour, and he often feels that it is an almost clairvoyant sense of the approaching form which provides him with the theme. Sometimes, indeed, a poet may begin with an entirely technical problem and rely upon it to stimulate his poetic faculties. Louis MacNeice once told me that he used sometimes to set himself the task of writing in a particular metre in the knowledge that the metre itself would somehow 'hypnotize' him and allow images and lines to come intuitively to him. Paul Valéry's poem, *Le Cimetière marin*, began as a sense of form. He wrote

> My own poem, *Le Cimetière marin* came to me in the form of a certain rhythm which is that of the ten-syllable French line arranged in the proportion of 4 to 6. I had not, at first, the slightest idea what content was to fill that form. Gradually, a number of floating words began to solidify. Little by little they determined my subject, and the labour (a very long labour) of composition was forced upon me. Another poem, *La Pythie,* began with an eight-syllable line the sound of which came of itself.[4]

Dylan Thomas would sometimes begin a poem by listing a series of rhymes and then construct the poem from there. For this he was criticized by Robert Frost, but Frost could not know, any more than we can, whether the rhyme selection preceded or followed the selection of a theme. Although in the twentieth century the spread of so-called 'free verse' and the increase in the number of prose-poems, has led many poets to feel that pre-selected form indicates a lack of integrity, a mere cleverness, it is interesting to note that one of the leaders of the 'free verse' movement was deeply interested in metrics.

In *Pavannes and Divisions* (1918), Ezra Pound wrote:

[1] ibid., p. 73.
[2] ibid., p. 100.
[3] ibid., p. 30.
[4] Paul Valéry, *Poetry and Abstract Thought*, translated by Gerard Hopkins (in *Essays on Language and Literature* ed. J. L. Hevesi, Wingate 1947, p. 109).

CREDO

Rhythm. I believe in an 'absolute rhythm', a rhythm, that is, in poetry which corresponds exactly to the emotion or shade of emotion to be expressed. A man's rhythm must be interpretative, it will be, therefore, in the end, his own, uncounterfeiting, uncounterfeitable.

Symbols. I believe that the proper and perfect symbol is the natural object, that if a man use 'symbols' he must so use them that their symbolic function does not obtrude; so that a sense, and the poetic quality of the passage, is not lost to those who do not understand the symbol as such, to whom, for instance, a hawk is a hawk.

Technique. I believe in technique as the test of a man's sincerity; in law when it is ascertainable; in the trampling down of every convention that impedes or obscures the determination of the law, or the precise rendering of the impulse.

Form. I think there is a 'fluid' as well as a 'solid' content, that some poems may have form as a tree has form, some as water poured into a vase. That most symmetrical forms have certain uses. That a vast number of subjects cannot be precisely, and therefore not properly rendered in symmetrical forms.

'Thinking that alone worthy wherein the whole art is employed'. I think the artist should master all known forms and systems of metric, and I have with some persistence set about doing this, searching particularly into those periods wherein the systems came to birth or attained their maturity. It has been complained with some justice, that I dump my note-books on the public. I think that only after a long struggle will poetry attain such a degree of development, or, if you will, modernity, that it will vitally concern people who are accustomed, in prose, to Henry James and Anatole France, in music to Debussy. I am constantly contending that it took two centuries of Provence and one of Tuscany to develop the media of Dante's masterwork, that it took the latinists of the Renaissance, and the Pleiade, and his own age of painted speech to prepare Shakespeare his tools. It is tremendously important that great poetry be written, it makes no jot of difference who writes it. The experimental demonstrations of one man may save the time of many—hence my furore over Arnaut Daniel—if a man's experiments try out one new rime, or dispense conclusively with one iota of currently accepted nonsense, he is merely playing fair with his colleagues when he chalks up his result.[1]

It is important to notice here that Pound considers that 'most symmetrical forms have certain uses' and that he believes that the poet 'should master all known forms and systems of metric'. Pound was, of

---

[1] *Literary Essays of Ezra Pound.* Faber 1954, pp. 9–10.

course, one of the great verse technologists, and his views may be considered untypical. Nevertheless other poets less generally regarded as
verse-technicians also reveal a deep concern with craftsmanship. Robert
Lowell said of the metrics of his collection, *Life Studies:*

> Most of it is free verse. But then that has to be specified. That there
> are four or five different ways I started a poem, roughly; that some,
> such as the 'Delmore Schwartz,' were written in perfectly regular
> meter and then taken out of that and irregularized and it once had two
> regular stanzas which disappeared. Bits of them remain in the poem
> and that was one extreme, and in fact, that even was quite a finished
> poem in regular meter which somehow never came off and I dug out of
> old manuscript. Then there are others where I wrote specifically at the
> time in regular meter and just felt they didn't work at all and ripped
> them up, like the Commander Lowell one. It was once a couplet poem
> and like 'Marble's Faun' it was perfectly regular. I just knocked it out
> but a lot of the couplets remain as rhymes. Then there were poems
> that were written in prose first and then were rewritten as poems. The
> 'Uncle Devereux', the first poem of the *Life Studies* series, was four or
> five prose pages that I rewrote into lines. And a poem like 'Home-
> coming' was written after I'd written a great deal in this meter where
> I'm deliberately—its first version was something like the final one,
> though much revised, but metrically the same—where I was trying to
> be lyrical and make the rhyme stand out and it was supposed to end a
> section and sound like a lyrical poem and it certainly shifts into iambic
> pattern which is the meter I'm most familiar with, yet it didn't—I
> didn't write it scanning. I was much more conscious of a metrical
> poem in the background. And then 'Skunk Hour', the last poem of
> the sequence was written in six-line stanzas where every line rhymes,
> though they're odd, off-rhymes, some of them. And then there's no
> meter within the line; they could be any length. And then there's
> even a poem like 'Man' and 'The Woe That Is in Marriage' and most
> of 'Man and Wife' which are perfectly regular metrical poems some-
> how meant to contrast with other poems. The free-verse poems—I
> think that the whole trick is that you've got to say to yourself, this
> isn't going to be scanned while you write it, that you're not given any
> rules. Then you may toss in little rhymes, or toss in lines where the
> beat is quite marked and an iambic line comes through. And if the
> iambic thing is too regular, you lose most of the advantages of free
> verse. That it ought to have rhythms that are not meant to be any way
> a wrenched, Donne-like iambic pentameter line. It just doesn't have
> any rules; it has that freedom.[1]

[1] Kenney Withers (ed.), *Conversations on the Craft of Poetry*. Holt, Rinehart and
Winston 1961, pp. 41–42.

John Crowe Ransom, Cleanth Brooks and Robert Penn Warren had an interesting exchange on the use a poet makes of his knowledge of metre and rhyme.

RANSOM: Well I'll mention two uses—one is technical—I know it well in my small experience as a poet. I think most poets who've written meters know it well. The first version of the poem that comes out just drives us wild—we *know* we've got a poem there, but it's like an untamed tiger; we haven't got him firmly. We haven't got him by the right place and we must do something about it—we must revise the poem. There's no way to revise a poem—and some young poets are without the capacity to do this which would indicate that they lack something of the gift of being a poet—without taking the very same situation, shutting our eyes, and submitting it again to the imagination to see what's there: to see if better little aspects, little angles, of that experience won't turn up. Well now, it's hopeless if you go out into the woods, say, and say well, I'll rewrite this poem. You sit down and ponder but the thing won't come back, and you don't know what you're looking for, really. But now suppose there are places where the meter is unsatisfactory—and there always are—the meter's too rough. Or sometimes it's too smooth and it's got to be roughened up in order to get that counterpoint. And so we're looking at it with a metrical consideration: Here are two words coming together which mustn't come together; here is a phrase of four words which doesn't make any meter at all—and the prose is so powerful in it that nothing would disturb it. And so we then think of verbal changes—and then verbal suggestions comes in; or we think of rhymes and then we can easily figure on other rhymes. And we may be sure that after we have tinkered with a poem to improve or perfect or establish its meters, that the thing we finally pick as our poem will not be merely metrically acceptable, but it will have powerful imaginative quality. We are looking at it from all angles, though our attention is concentrated on finding the metrical feature.

BROOKS: How would you explain that, John? Is it that the conscious mind, given a problem to work with—a metrical problem—there is a further continuing release of the unconscious in some kind of profitable way?

RANSOM: I think so.

WARREN: Let me hang on to this notion a little longer. You're thinking of meter and rhyme, such mechanical requirements of verse writing, as an asset to the poet, then. This is distinguished from the function it might have for the reader—this is the poet's profit in the business. It becomes a method, then, for him—a method to go more deeply into his subject—into himself in relation to the subject, is that it? Something of the sort?

RANSOM: Yes, that's very fine.

WARREN: That it's a matter of a method opening up the possibilities of association and suggestion, then, in the situation he is sitting at that moment trying to write a poem—is that it?

RANSOM: Yes, that's it.[1]

Neither Ransom nor Lowell are suggesting a 'programme' in the way Pound suggests one. Their approach is pragmatic. They suggest no absolute principles of composition. Many poets, have, however, set out the principles on which their own or others' poetry should be constructed, and the vast majority of poetic 'movements' and 'revolutions' have begun as a consequence of technical explorations. Wordsworth's decision to 'write in a selection of the language really used by men' was, from one point of view, a decision about technique. The early statements of surrealism were concerned with methods of making poetry as much as with philosophical principles. The poets usually grouped together under the label 'Black Mountaineers' followed, and still follow, a technical programme outlined by Charles Olson, and the earlier movement of Imagism began with a definite set of rules about the proper use of language.

Many individual poets set themselves technical problems and develop programmes of their own. William Carlos Williams busied himself with the exploration and development of the three-step line. W. S. Graham studied the three-stress line over a long period by keeping a journal whose every entry was written in this form, and eventually became so comfortable within this rigorous framework that he was able to create his magnificent poem *The Dark Dialogues*, using many of his journal entries as parts of it. C. M. Doughty and W. H. Auden both set themselves the task of writing verse according to the rules of rhythm and alliteration followed by Anglo-Saxon poets. Swinburne and Tennyson, both brilliant metrists, imitated many of the most complicated classical metres, though their most ingenious structures are not their best poems. Concern for the craft of verse goes hand in hand with concern for the full exploration and presentation of poetic vision, however, in all but those

---

[1] Kenney Withers, op. cit.

instances when the poet is deliberately studying versecraft for itself alone. This one can see very clearly if one examines the worksheets of the poets. Here are transcriptions of worksheets of poems by Kingsley Amis, James K. Baxter, Anne Sexton and Robert Francis, followed by photographic reproductions of Robert Graves' worksheets for his poem, *A Bracelet*.[1]

[1] Reproduced from *The Malahat Review*, numbers 4, 5, 6, 12, and 25. The University of Victoria, British Columbia, 1968–1973.

KINGSLEY AMIS: WORKSHEETS

If the poet is permitted comment, I would say that to take a poem through as many versions as I did with *South* has always turned out to mean, for me, that I started with the wrong form. And that I always feel fonder of a poem I have had to work at than one that came comparatively easily, though without necessarily feeling that the one is any better than the other.

I

```
To eyes half-shut against a bright sun
( No brighter, though, than seen in memory
( But no brighter than loving retrospect
  Saw the high summer sun
  But no brighter than, in dazed retrospect —
  The highest summer sun had shone on
                              England)
              ——    seemed
This land, too, must have looked like home
                              at first
Great gentle slopes thick with half-oak,
                              near-elm,
River-bends like the upper Thames
              an Avon magnified,
No palm or banyan, lumpish fruits,   fat
                                        flowers.
A winter that brought snow, not steaming
                              rain
Original England before the English
                              came.
```

II

To eyes half-shut against a bright sun
(But no brighter than, in dazed retrospect,
The extreme August sun had shone on England),

This land, too, must have seemed like home at first:
Great gentle slopes thick with half-oak, near-elm,
River-bends like an Avon magnified,

And creatures almost recognised

And creatures nearly known: the grey squirrel
Just larger than the red

And creatures nearly known: the blue jay screeched
Like a crow's cousin, and the grey squirrel
~~Was merely larger than~~ the red. ~~Nowhere~~ Far from here
         Had just outgrown

Those Horrible tall forests hung with fruit
That bulged and sweated, creepers thick as thighs,
Fat flowers that emblazoned Africa,

Nowhere painted birds, devilish apes

Were Those tall forests hung with fruit that bulged
And sweated, creepers thick as thighs, fat flowers
               s?
Dripping with venom, blazon of Africa;

Far too the painted birds, devilish apes
And worse, more human presences. Winter
Came there with warm rain, here with familiar snow.

III

This was the country of domesticated
Marvels
Wonders
Wonder ~~Marvels,~~ Nature's England before man came: Guns
No streets, guns, money, coaches, drink.   money
                                                                              roads   streets
There were men, but to any poet they   coaches
Must have seemed innocent   drink
                    free and innocent: these were   music
The woods through which the noble savage ran;

Wordsworth's rustics were born in Tennessee.

There were men, but here, to a poet, they

How sad, then, the inevitable shock
Of discord
     real savagery, money, guns.

Came there with warm rain, here with prosaic snow.

However non-innocent, the red man stayed
Free to the end

The red man never would have been a slave,
And became nothing. From a sickening land
Black damned wretches were brought to be miserable.
                                             do their part.

And something that would poison the future:
the final dying of that dream
                         sustaining
That man anywhere could be without sin

IV

To eyes half-shut against a bright sun
(But no brighter than, in dazed retrospect,
At summer's clearest noon had shone on England),

This land, too, must have seemed like home at first:
Great gentle slopes thick with half-oak, near-elm,
River-windings like Avon magnified,

And creatures nearly known: the blue jay yelled
Like a crow's cousin, and the grey squirrel
Was no more freakish than the red. Far off

Were those tall forests hung with fruit that sweated
And bulged, creeper thick as a thigh, fat flowers
Dripping with venom, blazons of Africa;

Far too the painted birds, devilish apes
And worse, more human presences. Winter
Came there with warm rain, here with prosaic snow.

This was the country of domesticated
Wonder, Nature's England before man came:
No streets, guns, money, coaches, drink.

There were men, but here, to a poet, they
Must have seemed free and innocent: these were
The woods through which the noble savage ran;

Wordsworth's rustics were born in Tennessee.
How sad, then, the inevitable shock
Of real savagery, money, guns,

And what would contaminate the future:
The absolute end of the old dream
That man anywhere could be without sin.

The redskin never would have been a slave,
And became nothing. From those vile jungles
Black damned wretches were brought to do their part.

end of part i

V

To eyes half-shut against a bright sun
(But no brighter than, in dazed retrospect,
At summer's clearest zenith shone on England),

This land, too, must have looked like home at first:
Great gentle slopes thick with half-oak, near-elm,
River-windings like Avon magnified,

And creatures nearly known: the blue jay yelled
Like a crow's cousin, and the grey squirrel
Bounded, stood still, and bounded, like the red.

This was the country of domesticated
Wonder, Nature's England before man came

VI

To eyes half-shut against a bright sun
(But no brighter than, in dazed retrospect,
At summer's clearest zenith shone on England),

This land, too, must have looked like home at first:
Great gentle slopes thick with half-oak, near-elm,
River-windings like Avon magnified,

And creatures nearly known: the blue jay yelled
Like a crow's cousin, and the grey squirrel
Bounded, stood still, and bounded, like the red,

But no hedges, no lines of growing wealth,
No thronged market streets with, at the end,

No clustered market streets with, at th

But no hedges, tende

No

But no hedges, careful rows of next year's wealth,
Chimneys, loud market streets with, at the end,
Bare   Masts and rigging tangled against ~~the~~ clouds,
                       guns
No gardens, coaches, money, ~~books,~~ drink.
Wonders forgotten and familiar
Lived here, in Nature's England without men.
                             before

There were men, but to any poet they
Must have seemed free and innocent: these were
The woods through which the noble savage ran.

Wordsworth's rustics were born in the south land.

And what   the long result

And what would

And that long destructive disappointment:
The end for ever of the old dream
That, somewhere,

The end for ever of the ancient hope
That, somewhere, man could be without skin.

There were men,v

VII

A burning sun

A sun like Africa, but the sky

A sun like noon in Sicily,
But a paler, gentle sky,
Sky-blue mostly.

Against

A sun as bright as noon in Sicily
Against a cool, transparent sky,
Sky-blue mostly.

Pre

Great gentle slopes thick with half-known trees,

Bluff, slip-off slope, oxbow lake, meander,
Enormous, but   some
            and yet like a river
Half a world from here.
A long way
Long gentle slopes thick with half-known trees

Oak and horse-chestnut among the half-unknown,

the history of ideas

The red squirrel's

A sort of squirrel, a crow's cousin,

Oak and horse-chestnut among half-unknown
Maple, dogwood; a squirrel's kin   the
     The crow's cousin.

hand grand sand stand withstand
reigned stained unchained ordained profaned explained
end bend
find mind wind mankind
sinned wind
dawned beyond
found round ground southbound

Old wonders recognied

New wonders recognised, old, unprofaned,
A world of difference without end,
     God's England.

age rage ~~damage~~ ridge bondage message ~~language~~ voyage
hermitage heritage parentage huge

Actual native of a golden age   the
Free of man's gloomy heritage,
     The noble savage.

VIII

A sun as bright as noon in Sicily
Against a ~~cool~~ transparent sky,
  Sky-blue mostly.

Bluff, slip-off slope, oxbow lake, meander,
Enromous, and yet like some river
  A long way from here.

Oak and horse-chestnut among half-unknown
Maple, dogwood; a squirrel's kin   the
  The crow's cousin.

New wonders recognised, old, unpro~~f~~aned,
A wo~~rld~~ of difference without end,
  God's England.

Actual na~~ti~~ve of the golden age,
F~~ree~~ of man's gloomy heritage:
  The noble savage,

                                           another country's
Hence the nativeXs of another country's   untrodden ways
Uplands, innocent

Later,

Far ancestor of another country's   But that was poetry
Innocent

IX

At any rate as seen from a distance.
And so, of course, Wordsworth's peasants
  In all innocence,

And, if you like, the man of the Just City,
Fabulously rich without money,
  And, perforce, free.

        *

The usual: ranch-style, eat-o-mat, drive-in,
1 Headlight, taillight, floodlight, neon,
   And air-pollution/ —

Except the last, ~~harmless~~?
All but

All but the last pretty innocuous?
Except the last,

2 But, through street after street, the voice   here alone
   Of something vicious.   no hope of
                                progress
Except the last, tolerable? Yes;

                          keep 'em out of midto
                          keep 'em down

4 If they try it I'm shooting me a coon. —
  Keep 'em out of uptown, midtown,—
   Keep 'em down.

             they got too much freedom

Already
3 You blind? Can't you see they're inferior? —
  Our women's what they're really after —
   You got to use fear —

          a bit more of the usual
Across the tracks — what need to   detail
The mad and understandable

                  in the libraries, books full
             6   of ideas
                  about innocence

           8 Something to share
     For everybody, ~~Lack of~~ future
               no
           Not Here

X

Across the tracks, a bit more of the usual:
Mad, ~~vain,~~ understandable   hopeless
  Design to kill.

In the libraries, books full of ideas
                  books about justice,
Freedom, ~~goodness~~ innocence, goodness.
  No use.

                    *

The history of thought is a side-issue.
When events begin, an idea
  Is a lie.

To the north and ~~the~~ west, hope of a kind;
                          something to hope for;
In Mexico too, and further;

To north and west, hope, not yet in vain;
Mexico too, not an illusion;
  Africa, even;

But for these people, just one thing to share:
                          new for
But in the South, nothing now or ever,
For black and white, no future,
  None. Not here.

Where the folks are happy and gay,
And the easy way is the right way.

I

II

The Vine
THE WINE JAR

        about   before the roof fell down
Up in Auckland — yes, twelve years ago   On Lowry's head —

               I'd
In Lowry's house — I had bought a peter of wine

From the owner of a Dalmatian vineyard,

And carried it with me wherever I went —

A simulacrum of the unobtainable breast,   Something to ease the jittery

Tasting of autumn and the roots of trees,   Something to have beside my bed in the
                                                   morning

A jug filled at the udders of the the sky!

And while some were nattering in the kitchen

And some were dancing down on the wooden floor

Of the middle room — half drunk, I held it up
               never
And saw what I had/hoped to see,

A picture of the impossible →

On the curve of the wine jar Dionysus was lying
            and asleep
Asleep, naked in a black boat,

With a beard like the waves of the sea — and out of his belly

A vine was growing, vine of ether, vine of earth,

Vine of water / growing towards a sky

Blue as the veins on the inside of a woman's arm —

Black boat, white belly, curved blue sky

Holding us in its hands, as if Heaven and Earth   and Heaven

Were the friends of man, not his enemies —

   picture   sat gripped
A vision of what is not, as I lay lulled by

The mad vine of drunkenness and sleep.

III

The Jar
THE VINE

Up in Auckland about twelve years ago

In Lowry's house — before the roof fell down

On Lowry's head — I'd bought a peter of wine

From the owner of a Dalmatian vineyard,

And carried it with me wherever I went —

Something to ease the jitters,

Something to have beside my bed in the morning —

And while some were nattering in the kitchen

And some were dancing down on the wooden floor

Of the middle room — half drunk, I held it up,

And saw what I had never ~~hoped to see~~ —   even thought of

On the curve of the wine jar Dionysus was lying

Naked and asleep in a black boat,

With a beard like the waves of the sea — and out of his belly

A vine growing, vine of ether, vine of earth,

Vine of water — growing towards a sky

Blue as the veins on the inside of a woman's arm —

Black boat, white belly, curved blue sky

Holding us in its hands, as if Earth and Heaven

Were the friends of man, not his enemies —

                can't be
A picture of what ~~is not,~~ as I sat gripped by

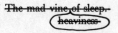

~~The mad vine of sleep.~~
      (~~heaviness~~)

The mad, heavy vine of sleep .

The Jar

Up in Auckland about twelve years ago
In Ivan's house — before the roof fell down
On Ivan's head — I'd bought a peter of wine
From the owner of a Dalmatian vineyard,
And carried it with me wherever I went —
Something to ease the jitters,
Something to have beside my bed in the morning —

And while some were nattering in the kitchen
And some were dancing down on the wooden floor
Of the middle room — half drunk, I held it up,
And saw what I had never even thought of —

On the curve of the wine jar Dionysus lying
Naked and asleep in a black boat,
With a beard like the waves of the sea — and out of his belly
A vine growing, vine of ether, vine of earth,
Vine of water — growing towards a sky
Blue as the veins on the inside of a woman's arm —

Black boat, white belly, curved blue sky
Holding us in its hands as if Earth and Heaven
Were the friends of man, permanent friends —

A picture of what can't be, as I sat gripped by
The mad, heavy vine of sleep.

ANNE SEXTON: WORKSHEETS

I

My skin's as old as a rug
that's been beaten down to its strings,
all my worn out and shabby years
rest

My skin's as old as a rug
that's been worn down to its strings,
and I walk in circles
over and over it

My skin's as old as a rug
that's been worn down to its strings . . .
Shabby but sufficient enough
to walk in circles over and over
my old defeats.

Come friend, I have an old story
to talk about; an old story that I
walk over and over in circles

Come friend, I have an old story
to tell you about, its been walked on
like a carpet that's worn down to its threads . . .
~~the~~ little fevorish roses ~~are worn down,~~
the island of olives and radishes)
are pale where my feet
the ~~b~~lishfull pastimes of the parlor
are beaten down to their strings.

II

Come friend, I have an old story
to tell you about, it's been walked on
like a carpet;
the little feverish roses,
the islands of olives and radishes,
the blishful pastimes of the parlor
    all
are/worn down to their colorless threads.
Listen, sit beside me and listen.
Liquor is my strong arm,
my face is red with sorrow
and my breasts are made of straw.
Who wants my skin?   It's as old as the rug
and the story, itself, is older,
less usefull, covering nothing I remember.
it won't keep you warm.
I was a wall flower, see how
boring that is!   And what's more
I'm still pacing up and down that rug.
I herewith forgive the actors for dying.
I stole their lines,
but it's an old story
fastidious and precise.
It's still in my mouth.
It's no good either,
never you mind,
who wants it anyhow.

III

WALLFLOWER —

~~A BAD POEM THAT I WROTE ANYHOW~~

Come friend, I have an old story
to tell you, it's been walked on
like a carpet;
the little feverish roses,
the islands of olives and radishes,
the blishfull pastimes of the parlor
are worn down to the colorless threads.
Listen.
Sit down beside me and listen.
~~Liquor is my strong arm.~~
~~I am dressed like a wallflower,~~
my face is red with sorrow
and my breasts are made of straw.
I'm pacing up and down on the rug.
I have forgiven all the other actors for dying.
I have stolen their lines.   They are in my mouth.
Now I am catching, a chill my thighs scrape
gently below their treasure.
My hands wash off my disease
and how I came to this place
I'll never know
~~nevermind,~~
~~who wants it anyhow.~~

IV

WALLFLOWER

Come friend,
I have an old story to tell you,
it's been walked on like a carpet;
the little feverish roses,
the islands of olives and radishes
the blishfull pastimes of the parlor
are worn down to their rough threads.
Listen.   Sit down beside me and listen.
My face is red with sorrow
and my breasts are made of straw.
I am pacing in circles on ~~that rug.~~ *the stage.*
I am wearing it out.
I have forgiven all the other actors for dying.
because Their lines are in my mouth.
Perhaps I am catching a chill.
My thighs scrape, holding up their treasure.
My hands wash off my disease
and how I came to this place
I'll never know.

> *Upstage*
> *the fat man*
> *stirs the*
> *fire —*

V

WALLFLOWER

Come friend,
I have an old story to tell you,
it's been walked on like a carpet,
the little feverish roses,
the islands of olives and radishes,
the blishfull pastimes of the parlor
are worn down to their rough threads.
Listen.   Sit down beside me and listen.
My face is red with sorrow
and my breasts are made of straw.
I am sitting in a ladder-back chair
in the corner of the empty stage.
I have forgiven all the old actors for dying
because new ones come on with the same lines
in their mouth.   It's like a dance I went to once.
My hands twists in my lap.   I look up.
The ceiling is pearly

because their lines are

be

New ones come on with the same lines in their mouth.

New ones come on with the same lines,
like overgrown pearls, in their mouth.

A new one comes on with the samelines,
like overgrown pearls, in his mouth.

Anne

73

VI

WAllflower

Come friend,
I have an old story to tell you,
it's been walked on like a carpet,
the little feverish roses,
the islands of olives and radishes,
the blissful pastimes of the parlor
are worn down to their rough threads.
Listen.   Sit down beside me and listen.
My face is red with sorrow
and my breasts are made of straw.
I sit in the ladder-back chair
in the corner of the empty stage.
I have forgiven all the old actors for dying.
A new one comes on with the samelines,
like large white growths, in his mouth.
It's like a dance I went to once.
I look up.   The ceiling is pearly.
My thighs press, holding in their treasure.
Upstage a bride falls in satin to the floor.
Beside her the hero in his red wool robe
stirs the fire with his cane.
The dancers come on from the wings,
perfectly mated.
My hands wash off my disease
and how I came to this place
I'll never know.
I have the same lines in my mouth,
like large white growths.

WALLFLOWER

Come friend,
I have an old story to tell you,
it's been walked on like a carpet,
the little feverish roses,
the islands of olives and radishes,
the blissfull pastimes of the parlor
are worn down to their rough threads.

Listen.
Sit down beside me and listen.
My face is red with sorrow
and my breasts are made of straw.
I sit in the ladder-backed chair
in the corner of the plished stage.
I have forgiven all the old actors for dying.
A new one comes on with the same lines,
like large white growths, in his mouth.
The dancers come on from the wings,
perfectly mated.

I look up.   The ceiling is pearly.
My thighs press, ~~holding~~ in their treasure.   *knotting*
Upstage the bride falls in satin to the floor.
Beside her the tall hero in his red wool robe
stirs the fire with his cane.

The string quartett play for each other,
up and down, sleeves and waxy bows.
   legs of the
The dancers leap and catch.

I myself, as straight as a book,
but how I came to this place,
I'll never know.

VIII

WALLFLOWER

~~Oh~~, that old story,
who wants it, it's a worn out rug,
thin, beaten down to the strings it was madeof
shabby somehow, where I walk in circles
of the old defeats.

somewhere in this desk
under the old twenty dollar bill,
under the crhistmas letter i never answered,
. . . . my mothers picture,
her face fat with her death,
her last smile perhaps . . .

~~what is still~~

she ~~what~~ keeps going on in me
~~is them~~ . . .
I can forgive you for dying . . .
but not for the birth . . .
just like him
I m getting drunk
to turn ~~off~~ myself . off . . .
liquor is my strong arm
my face is made of straw,
the bodies of the dead have faded,
the needs of the dead ~~reamin,~~ remain,
fastidious,
civil,
constant, in my mouth.
Nevermind,
it's no good,
never you mind,
who wants it,
no one.

WALLFLOWER

Jan 2 - 3rd
1962

Come friend,
I have an old story to tell you,
~~it's been walked on like a carpet,~~
the little feverish roses,
the islands of olives and radishes,
the blissful pastimes of the parlor
are worn down to their rough threads.

Listen/ Sit down beside me and listen.
My face is red with sorrow
and my breasts are made of straw.
I sit in the ladder-backed chair
in the corner of the polished stage.
I have forgiven all the old actors for dying.
A new one comes on with the same lines,
like large white growths, in his mouth.
The dancers come on from the wings,
perfectly mated.

I look up. The ceiling is pearly.
My thighs press, knotting in their treasure.
Upstage the bride falls in satin to the floor.
Beside her the tall hero in ~~his~~ a red wool robe
stirs the fire with his ivory cane.
The string quartett plays for ~~each other,~~ *itself*
gently, gently, sleeves and waxy bows.
The legs of the dancers leap and catch.
~~I myself, am straight as a book,~~
~~with little stiff legs, a neck like a husk,~~
~~head down, my heart tearing the skirts~~
~~off the dancers,~~
~~that holds my eye angry eyes.~~

I myself, have little stiff legs,
&, my back's as straight as a book
& how I came to this place
I'll never know —

X

Wallflower

Come friend,
I have an old story to tell you —

Listen.
Sit down beside me and listen.
My face is red with sorrow
and my breasts are made of straw.
I sit in the ladder-back chair
in a corner of the polished stage.
I have forgiven all the old actors for dying.
A new one comes on with the same lines,
like large white growths, in his mouth.
The dancers come on from the wings,
perfectly mated.

I look up.   The ceiling is pearly.
My thighs press, knotting in their treasure.
Upstage the bride falls in satin to the floor.
Beside her the tall hero in a red wool robe
stirs the fire with his ivory cane.
The string quartet plays for itself,
gently, gently, sleeves and waxy bows.
The legs of the dancers leap and catch.
I myself have little stiff legs,
my back is as straight as a book
and how I came to this place —
the little feverish roses,
the islands of olives and radishes,
the blissful pastimes of the parlour —
I'll never know.

*From Anne Sexton: *All My Pretty Ones*, Houghton Mifflin, 1962.

78

ROBERT FRANCIS: WORKSHEETS

I   April 5, 1946

Who is the hawk whose squeal

Is like a child's toy wound

And suddenly let loose

     in whirling wheels.

And why this warming sound

When silence would be

     deathlier?

But why ask why or whose

II

Who is the hawk whose squeal

Is like a child's toy wound

And suddenly let loose

In disengaging wheels?

And why this warning sound

When none would be deathlier

And why?   Why any sound

When none would be deathlier?

Who is the hawk whose squeal

Is like a child's toy wound

And suddenly let loose

In disengaging wheels?

And why the warning?   Why

The silent wings, the cry?

Any

III

        Who? Why?

Who is the hawk whose squeal

Is like a child's toy wound
Then
And suddenly let loose

In disengaging wheels?

And why the warning cry?
            sound
Why any cry at all
Since   in
When death does best to fall   ing

Silent if not unseen?

IV   Evening

        Who?   Why?

Who is the hawk whose squeal

Is like the shivering sound

Of a too-tightly wound

Child's toy that slips a wheel?

And why the warning cry?

Why any sound at all

Since death does best to fall

Silently from the sky?

V

Who? Why?

Who is the hawk whose squeal

Is like the shivering s/hound

Of a too-tightly wound

Child's toy that slips a wheel?

And why the warning cry?
        sound
Why any ~~cry~~ at all

When death has skill to fall
      a
Silent from the clear sky?

VI   April 7, 1946

Suffern, N.Y.

Who is the hawk whose squeal

Is like the shivering sound

Of a too-tightly wound

Child's toy that slips a reel?

And since death

But Beyond ~~the~~ who is why?

Why any sound at all

When death has but to fall
      a
Silently from the sky?

Soundlessly the

Who is the hawk whose squeal

Is like the shivering sound

Of a too tightly wound

Child's toy that slips a reel?

But beyond who is why,

Why any cry at all

When death knows how to fall

Soundless from the sky?

April 9, 1946 Fort Juniper

The Hawk

and

~~Who? Why?~~

Who is the hawk whose squeal

Is like the shivering sound

Of a too tightly wound

Child's toy that slips a reel?

But beyond who is why.

Why any cry at all

Since death knows how to fall

Soundlessly from the sky?

The Hawk

Who is the hawk whose squeal
Is like the shivering sound
Of a too tightly wound
Child's toy that slips a reel?

But beyond who is why.
Why any cry at all
Since death knows how to fall
Soundlessly from the sky?

From Robert Francis: *Come Out Into The Sun, Poems New and Selected*, The University of Massachusetts Press, 1965.

Moon
~~Browface,~~
~~Heartface~~
~~Sunface~~, accept of me.
A ~~this~~ bracelet invisible

For you busy wrist:
~~It's forged Hammered your~~ ~~you~~
~~Hammered~~ from ~~tooth~~ silver
~~In the~~ On a still night:

Eight and twenty moonlets
Sent to surprise you
Waxing and waning,
~~In~~ A ~~chain~~ ~~circuit chain~~ complete.
It is ~~monsters forge harness~~
~~And creating magic~~
To ~~mountains to~~ [behaviourment] ~~the wolf~~ evil-eye
By ~~the dearest off~~ Hammered [demons] the evil-so ~~leave~~
Of your ~~strong~~ stray ~~pulses~~ beat. By many of her
(true pulse beat.

O moon
Soon fall, accept of me wear in
These bracelet invisible
On your busy arm:
From your lunar
silver
till evening
Eight and twenty moonlets
Sent to surprise you,

Waxing and waning,
to their chain complete.

By the evil law
Of your true pulse beat.
For your firm

Moonface ~~pray wear this~~
~~wear to~~

~~This~~ Bracelet invisible:

Twenty-eight lunulas

Sent ~~be jingling~~

On a brazy arm :
~~It was~~ wear it as a charm

~~forgot~~ him moon silver

At ~~one~~ a still ~~evening~~
~~Is a nothing~~ absence.   ~~midnight night~~

~~Here I~~

Wear ~~it~~ ~~a certain~~ charm

High ~~of mounting~~ magic
~~that~~ that will ~~Events~~ ~~times~~
~~who Schemes~~

Solemnly to infuse you us

But ~~may~~ us ~~you~~ harm .

Accept, ~~sweet~~   Accept of
~~Sweet~~ Moon Face,   ~~from me~~
~~Has bracelet~~ invisible,   A bracelet invisible
Twenty-eight ~~moonlets~~ hundreds
Sent ~~to~~ ~~be you weary~~ ~~surprise you~~

~~So~~ ~~for a~~ On ~~you~~
~~free~~ ~~busy~~ arm

~~They are~~ forged from ~~lunar~~ silver
In ~~one a~~ month ~~of nights~~ of ~~~~ absent
Waxing ~~to very to want~~,
On then
~~La so~~ chain of ~~silver~~
~~A certain~~ charm ~~~~, there is a ~~~~ certain

Of ~~monotonous~~ magic
I ~~that will~~
to constrain demons
Who ~~schemes~~ to confuse you
And bring you harm.

87

O Noon Face, wear for me
~~This~~ My bracelet invisible
On your busy arm
Forged from moon silver
In one still night.
To a ~~loss~~ ~~explain~~ ~~might~~ charm
~~moontang~~ ~~tivoli's~~
~~certain~~
Twenty-eight ~~moonbits~~ lunulae
Sent to ~~respiration~~
~~Waxing & waning,~~
~~Their chains complete~~ Running
A mountain They.
~~A no constant~~ magic
To counter demons
Who scheme to ~~disorder~~ confuse you
~~Your from pulse beat~~
And bring ~~old~~ harm.

Moonface, they wear this
Bracelet invisible.
Twenty-eight ~~lunulas~~ ~~butterflies~~ ~~little bats~~.
Sent you for jingling
On your busy arm.
Wear it for a charm.
It was ~~forged out~~ from you silver
One still cool evening:
~~High~~ magic
That ~~will~~ counter demons
Selene to confuse us
And bring us harm.

A bracelet, invisible,
For your bony wrist
To start with your pulse beat.

Hammered from moon-silver
In the Smithy of night;

94

A bracelet invisible
For your busy wrist,
~~Forged from now~~ silver
In the ~~chill of~~ a still night :
~~Eight-and-twenty~~ minutes
Sent to treasure you,
~~Confounding~~ all demons
That ~~would obsess~~ ~~to trouble~~ ;
Let it pulse at your pulse .

From silver of the moon
~~From~~ ~~a~~ ~~street~~ function : long
~~to be full~~
~~Not to be~~

From ~~your~~ throbbing pulse .
Never ~~And the~~ scheming demons
Are ~~Fly off in~~ .
~~Driven to~~ flight
Things for

95

A Bracelet

A bracelet invisible
For your busy wrist,
Twisted from silver
Of a dull night full
From silver of the Moon,
From her sheer halo —
Has the solemn
From the sudden trail
Pale in their flight
Of the falling star

4

A BRACELET

A bracelet invisible

For your busy wrist,

Twisted from silver

Fetched from far,

From silver of the Moon,

From her sheer halo,

And the sudden glory

Of ~~your~~ natal star.

A bracelet invisible
On for your busy wrist
Twisted from silver
Of the a chill night :
From silver of the Moon,
From her sheer halo —
Here the scheming demons
Pale in their flight .

A Bracelet

A bracelet invisible for your busy wrist,
Twisted from silver of a chill night,
From silver of the full Moon, from her sheer halo :
Here the scheming demons pale in their flight .

A BRACELET

A bracelet invisible
For your busy wrist,
Twisted from silver
Of a chill night: *Spilt afar*
From silver of the Moon,
From her sheer halo
Here the scheming demons
Pale in their flight.
From ... the ... clear beauty
Of a falling star *Shooting star.*

A BRACELET

A bracelet invisible
For your busy wrist,
Twisted from silver
Spilt afar,
From silver of the *clear* Moon,
From her sheer halo,
From the ~~made~~ beauty
Of a shooting star.

98

A Bracelet

A bracelet invisible
For your busy wrist,
Twisted for silver
Spilt afar,
From silver of the clear Moon,
From her sheer halo,
From the male beauty
Of a shooting star.

from *Poems 1965-1968*
Doubleday & Company Inc.
Baillière, Tindall & Cassell Ltd.

FIVE A Learned Difficult Art

So far I have been discussing the pursuit of poetry as if it were, in general, a somewhat unintellectual activity. I have made it appear that the poet may have to be a clever and conscious craftsman, but the content of his poetry is discovered intuitively and often during the act of writing the poem and is not the result of deliberate philosophical speculation. This is, of course, a half truth. Poets come to their poems with an ever-increasing store of memories (what James Dickey has called 'a memory bank'), and some of these memories are of ideas and philosophical speculations and not only of personal experiences. 'Any given poem' Dickey told John Graham, 'is a collaboration between the poet and his memory bank.'[1] The dedicated poet is a person who deliberately creates memories to place in this bank. He will travel, he may visit new or strange places, explore new experiences, meet new people in other walks of life. He will also read widely, and sometimes deeply. James Dickey, talking of his poem, *Falling*, said

> . . . in that poem I wanted to use a kind of Bergsonian time shift, in which time itself, that is as we know it, clock time, would not be real time. What we have in that poem is what Bergson referred to as *duree*, duration, lived time, rather than clock time, where things seem to stretch out longer than they ordinarily would.[2]

While we, the readers, do not need to read Bergson to understand or be moved by James Dickey's poem, it seems clear that Dickey himself found that the presence of Bergson in his memory bank either helped him to write or even set him to writing it. Other poets reveal the same kind of intellectual background in their discussions of their poems, or even in the poems themselves. In his notes to his long poem, *New Year Letter*, W. H. Auden quotes from Nietzsche, Wolfgang Kohler, Pascal, Kierkegaard, R. G. Collingwood, Jacques Maritain, Spinoza, Georg Groddeck, Voltaire, and a host of other philosophers, anthropologists,

[1] George Garrett (ed.), *The Writer's Voice: Conversations With Contemporary Writers conducted by John Graham*. William Morrow and Co. 1973, p. 236.
[2] ibid., p. 230.

psychologists, historians, poets, novelists, and playwrights. Auden is, perhaps, an extreme case: his knowledge was encyclopaedic and, being frequently a didactic poet, he was often concerned to present material that is (if one may be permitted a shaky distinction) more philosophical than poetic. Nevertheless, even Robert Frost, whose prose, in conversation, was almost invariably that of a man who had no intellectual or philosophical pretensions, admitted that his memory bank had been enriched by many deposits of learned knowledge.

INTERVIEWER: I've been asking a lot of questions about the relationship of your poetry to other poetry, but of course there are many other non-literary things that have been equally important. You've been very much interested in science, for example.

FROST: Yes, you're influenced by the science of your time, aren't you? Somebody noticed that all through my book there's astronomy.

INTERVIEWER: Like 'The Literate Farmer and the Planet Venus'?

FROST: Yes, but it's all through the book, all through the book. Many poems—I can name twenty that have astronomy in them. Somebody noticed that the other day: 'Why has nobody ever seen how much you're interested in astronomy?' That's a bias, you could say. One of the earliest books I hovered over, hung around, was called *Our Place Among the Infinities*, by an astronomer in England named Proctor, noted astronomer. It's a noted old book. I mention that in one of the poems: I use that expression 'our place among the infinities' from that book that I must have read as soon as I read any book, thirteen or fourteen, right in there I began to read. . . .[1]

Frost's description of this book as one that he 'hovered over, hung around' expresses extremely well the way in which poets tend to read quite a number of books. While they may study some subject closely, explore some particular philosophy in depth, as Kathleen Raine studied Jung and Neo-Platonism, and as Yeats studied Hermetic Philosophy, they are certain also to have other books which they dip into, browse through, and allow to stimulate them. Susan Musgrave told me:

I read a lot of things in the library here. There's a thing called the

[1] George Plimpton (ed.), *Writers at Work. The Paris Review Interviews, Second Series*. The Viking Press 1965, pp. 22–23.

Journal of American Folklore—hundreds of volumes—and I love just pulling one out and turning to any page and reading what's on it, and often there will be some interesting word or some strange name which will start a poem, and that's the sort of thing I read for.

I myself often follow a similar procedure. Though by no means a serious student of pre-Socratic Greek philosophy I have been dipping into it for years, and many of my poems have begun with a hint from Herakleitos or Empedokles. I do not wish to study these philosophers too thoroughly; systematic exploration leading to a thorough understanding would, I feel, tend to inhibit me in my imaginative responses to these fragments of poetry and wisdom. I would *know* what Herakleitos meant (or know what the commentators *say* he meant) and might well find myself blocked from developing an intuitive response to his thought. On the other hand, I have read all of Jung that has been translated into English and a good many books about his work and by his followers. Jung is, for me, a thinker who raises questions as often as he answers them, and whose thought does not evolve in the direction of a closed system which limits the possibilities of further exploration.

Many poems have their beginnings in the *aperçus* of other writers, and many are prefaced by quotations which indicate the poet's interest in tackling a theme which he has discovered in the work of some psychologist, philosopher, or historian. Many poets write poems about figures of the past. Edith Sitwell constructed a series of poems on the *Casket Letters* of Mary Queen of Scots: James Elroy Flecker, John Heath-Stubbs and Sidney Keyes are but three of the many twentieth-century poets who have written of Don Juan. Many poems have been written about Saints, Roman Emperors, and other historical figures, and about other and earlier poets. Some poets have even chosen to remake, or reinterpret, earlier works of literature; there is the *Hamlet of Archibald MacLeish*, for example, and earlier literature is filled with the retellings of tales originating in Boccaccio, and the folk tales of medieval Europe.

All this may reveal the poet to be something of a magpie, an Autolycus, a 'snapper up of unconsidered trifles' and this, indeed, he is. He is also, however, sometimes a systematic collector who is concerned to make poems which, when brought together, create a coherent view of intellectual and social history, or at least an over-all attitude towards human experience of the past as of the present. Poetry synthesizes; it brings past and present together; it attempts, finally, an over-all view of the human condition, and those who are bent upon serving Poetry to the utmost will pursue both their casual and their systematic 'collecting', their watchful browsings and their serious studies, in such a way that they can furnish their memory banks with sufficient capital to feel equal to investing in an epic, a long philosophical poem, or poem-sequence of real intellectual substance. In the twentieth century we have seen several poets attempt this. Pound gave us his *Cantos*, William Carlos Williams his *Paterson*, and Charles Olson his *Maximus* poems, all of which testify to memory-banks of formidable size. Eliot summed up a philosophy in his shorter *Four Quartets*; Wallace Stevens presented his comprehensive philosophy in *Notes Towards a Supreme Fiction* and Hugh MacDiarmid wrote *The Drunk Man Looks at a Thistle* and *In Memoriam James Joyce*. W. H. Auden presented us with several major poems of length, including *New Year Letter*, *The Sea and the Mirror*, and *The Age of Anxiety*. Walter de la Mare gave us, towards the end of his life, *Winged Chariot*. Louis MacNeice produced *Autumn Journal* and *Autumn Sequel*, and Archibald MacLeish the long narrative poem, *Conquistador*. More recently John Montague has summed up the history, culture, and agony of Ulster in *The Rough Field*, and Peter Russell has completed his epic, *Ephemeron*.

I make this list to indicate that, while it is commonly stated that 'the epic is dead' and that the day of the long poem is over, the last fifty years has produced almost as considerable a number of significant long poems as did any other fifty-year period in our history.

Not all poets attempt the long comprehensive poem, of course, and those who do so face many problems, both psychological and technical. They also, before they even begin work on their magnus opus, are obliged to spend a great deal of time on preparatory studies, and on reorganizing the material in the memory bank and adding to it. No man can, however, call easily to mind all that he wishes or needs to remember while planning or working on a major creation, and thus the ambitious poet is obliged to organize for himself a library suitable to his purpose. It is not commonly realized that many poets, and all poets who attempt large-scale creations, are among the most assiduous collectors of reference works. Both Robert Graves (whose short poems of the last twenty years form a coherent and ever-developing pattern) and W. H. Auden, who frequently tackled large-scale creation, have spoken of the importance of possessing the multi-volume *New English Dictionary*, together with its supplements. No poet that I know would be without a *Roget's Thesaurus*; the majority also possess foreign language dictionaries, dictionaries of slang, and, indeed, almost any book they have been able to lay their hands on that deals with words and etymology. The study of language is not, however, sufficient. One must also study images, symbols, and myths. It is important to be able to recognize the various possible significances of the images that leap, apparently unprompted, into the mind, and to get a working knowledge of those symbols which have appeared over and over again in world literature. Thus, the poet's bookshelves are likely to contain Frazer's *Golden Bough* (preferably in the multi-volume edition), various works on Classical mythology, including Robert Graves's two volume Penguin study, and works dealing with the mythologies of many countries. It is necessary also for the poet to be able to check allusions that come to his mind, and to have books which enable him to make use of references to the past without committing serious errors. He is likely, therefore, to possess an Encyclopaedia, a Dictionary of Dates, and perhaps even a biographical dictionary. In addition to all this, if he is wise, he will possess Saintsbury's *History of English Prosody* (the one volume edition will do), Fowler's *English Usage*, Walker's *Terminological Dictionary* and at least one Dictionary of Quotations, together with Concordances to Shakespeare and the Bible. This, at least, is my own list of essentials. Few poets would disagree with me, though not all are able to possess a reference shelf of these proportions. Some poets would add other works to this list. I myself find Graves' *White Goddess* essential to me, and Graves' own library includes many classical volumes and chronicles including John Skelton's translation of *Diodorus Siculus*. Every poet has his own list of indispensable books.

The point I am making is that the poet who wishes to pursue his vocation with proper assiduity and responsibility needs just as many tools as the scholar, and may, indeed, need more, for his explorations are not limited to any one area of human endeavour or to the study and interpretation of any one period of history, or any single field of human knowledge. Though he may lack the narrow erudition of the specialist scholar, he must not be unlearned. He must be widely read, and preferably in history, philosophy, and psychology as well as world literature. He must not be totally ignorant of the sciences or of current affairs, and he must be adequately grounded in all the arts.

You will notice that I used the word 'must' and thus betrayed the fact that I am rather presenting an ideal programme than describing an actual situation. Nevertheless, even though some poets of established reputation would consider the programme ambitious, I do not believe that any but a small minority of modish primitives and devotees of the demotic would deny its validity.

In thus referring to those who consider that an outcry is invariably an insight, and who alter Wordsworth's dictum to read 'a selection of the language used by children and underprivileged adolescents' I am, of course, revealing, not for the first time, my bias towards the belief in poetry as a dignified and learned profession, a 'high mystery', rather than a trivial game of emotional assertion and vulgar pretension. If poetry is to be taken seriously, it must be made responsibly. There can be no end to the enriching of the memory bank, to the refining of technique, and to the process of exploration and study. Kathleen Raine, in commenting upon the superficiality and intellectual nullity of much present-day poetry, commented:

> It's awfully easy to set your sights too low in a society which is dedicated, perhaps rightly, to raising the level of the lowest by more widespread education, better living conditions and so on, which very much wishes, for the time being, to turn its back on the fact that there are the Prosperos as well as the Calibans to be considered.

I asked her to what extent she felt it important for a poet to be a philosopher, to have built up a kind of scholarship.

> It hasn't necessarily to be scholarship, but it must be something. You must have built up a great body of knowledge which may include many elements. It may include—I think it should include—scholarship; it should include experience of life and death, science, nature, religion—whatever goes to make human life. You should be building up. You see, Man has certain maximal possibilities and none of us reach that maximum, but poets, musicians, are, in a way, athletes of the spirit who are attempting to get a little further, to advance our humanity somewhat in the direction of what we might become.

I have already indicated some of the ways in which poets 'attempt to get a little further' and enlarge their fund of useable information, their bank of images, ideas, and facts. There is, however, another, and one which has become of increasing importance during the present century when communications between countries has increased and more and more people think in terms of world literature rather than in terms of the literature of their own particular country. This is, of course, translation. Many poets feel that it is important to broaden their understanding of poetic modes and attitudes by studying the work of writers in other languages. To a poet the only thorough way to study the poetry of a foreign writer is to attempt to translate it, to learn its nature so well that it is possible to bring that nature over into another tongue. Some poets are scholar-translators who pride themselves upon the precision with which they reproduce the rhythmical effects and exact sense of the original. Others are rather adapters than translators, more eager to make a new, and splendid, poem in English that retains the general character of the original, than to present an accurate phrase-by-phrase transcript. In between these two kinds of poet-translator are many who vary the degree of freedom with which they treat the foreign text, sometimes providing free versions and sometimes accurate ones. Not all the poets who explore foreign poetry in this fashion know the language from which they are translating. Like the translators of many oriental works in the nineteenth century, who quite frequently worked from an intermediary French text, they work from a prose translation provided by a friendly scholar or (if they are working on older poets) published in some scholarly edition such as the Loeb Library. To these prose versions they often add any other verse translations that have been published, and thus start work with several versions of the original in front of them. When they have made what seems to them a satisfactory poem they submit it to the criticism of a scholar in the original language, or even (if their subject is alive and bilingual) to the author's own scrutiny. A great many important works have been translated in this fashion, and have thus become part of the stock of poetry in English. Donald Davie (who knows no Polish) has provided us with a brilliant English adaptation of the *Pan Tadeusz* of Mickiewicz, using the Everyman prose version as his basic authority, and Stanley Kunitz has given us an incredibly elegant and moving translation of Akhmatova with the assistance of Max Hayward who is a more thorough scholar of Russian. Some of the most interesting adaptations have come from Robert Lowell who called his versions *Imitations* and made them with the avowed purpose, not of providing faithful translations, but of creating new poems as the consequence of a kind of dialogue between himself and the original writer. He said in his Preface to *Imitations*: 'I have tried to write alive English and to do what my authors might have done if they were writing now and in America' He admits

My licences have been many. My first two Sappho poems are really new poems based on hers. Villon has been somewhat stripped; Hebel is taken out of dialect; Hugh's 'Gautier' is cut in half. Mallarmé has been unclotted, not because I disapprove of his dense medium but because I saw no way of giving it much power in English. The same has been done with Ungaretti and some of the more obscure Rimbaud. About a third of 'The Drunken Boat' has been left out. Two stanzas have been added to Rilke's 'Roman Sarcophagus', and one to his 'Pigeons'. 'Pigeons' and Valéry's 'Helen' are more idiomatic and informal in my English. Some lines from Villon's 'Little Testament' have been shifted to introduce his 'Great Testament'. And so forth! I have dropped lines, moved lines, moved stanzas, changed images and altered meter and intent.

Pasternak has given me special problems. From reading his prose and many translations of his poetry, I have come to feel that he is a very great poet. But I know no Russian. I have rashly tried to improve on other translations, and have been helped by exact prose versions given me by Russian readers. This is an old practice; Pasternak himself, I think, worked this way with his Georgian poets. I hope I caught something worthy of his all-important tone.[1]

The next paragraph of the Introduction makes an important point for Lowell tells us, 'This book was written from time to time when I was unable to do anything of my own.' Lowell is not alone in this. My own translations of poems in the Greek Anthology and of Corbière began as ways to cope with an uncreative period, and many of David Gascoyne's translations of French poetry were made at a time when he could not write anything of his own. Translation is thus not only a deliberate—for it cannot be anything else—attempt to enlarge one's sensibility and to study the techniques and attitudes of other poets, but also a mode of keeping the creative machinery in action at a time when it might otherwise seize up altogether and lead to unbearable frustration and tension.

Translation is an exploration in many directions, of course. In translating Baudelaire one is not exploring the same techniques as in translating Horace; in attempting to translate Octavio Paz one will make discoveries quite different from those made in translating anyone else. One may, indeed, attempt to translate a particular poet in order fully to understand a particular technique which can then be used in one's own work. I suspect that it was Patrick Creagh's translations of Corbière that enabled him to give his later poetry that brilliant incisiveness and tough texture which makes it so remarkable, and it is perfectly obvious that Carolyn Kizer's translations from the Chinese have enabled her to enrich her own work with many delicate and dramatic effects.

The discoveries that poets make by means of their translations are of many kinds. Sometimes a certain tone of voice may be what they discover, as T. S. Eliot discovered one in Laforgue. Sometimes one may discover a new series of images, or a new way of handling a metaphor. Sometimes it may be that one discovers a totally new structure, a new poetic form, and is then able to make this form over into English as

---

[1] Robert Lowell, *Imitations*. Noonday Press 1962, p. 12.

Surrey and Wyatt made over the Italian Sonnet in the sixteenth century, and as others have made over into English the French Villanelle and Rondeau, the Japanese Haiku, and the Malayan Pantoum. One of the most interesting of recent innovations of this kind was the introduction of Welsh verse forms into English by the American poet and translator Rolfe Humphries. He discovered the rules for the twenty-four official Welsh meters in Gwyn Williams' fascinating book, *Introduction to Welsh Poetry*, and then in his own collection of poetry *Green Armour on a Green Ground* (1956) proceeded to use the rules to make English verse. One of the most interesting forms, (which seems, incidentally, to have been used before by Herrick in the seventeenth century) is the Rhupunt. Humphries describes the Rhupunt as 'a line of three, four or five sections of four syllables each. All but the last section rhyme with each other; the last section carries the main rhyme. Each section may be written as a separate line.' Rolfe Humphries' Rhupunt reads:

Winter, Old Style
(Rhupunt)

Keen is the wind,
Barren the land.
A man could stand.
On a single stalk.

Cattle are lean,
The stag is thin,
All color wan
On the frozen lake.

Idle the shield
On an old man's shoulder.
Halls are cold.
I have a wound.

Where warriors go
I cannot follow
Through flying snow
In this wild wind.

The trees are bowed
In the bare wood;
There is no shade
in any vale.

The reeds are dry
And a loud crying
Howls outside
The horse's stall.

The light is short.
Sorrow and hurt
Harry the heart
With inward war.

So an old man
Does what he can,
Stares through the pane
At night's black square.[1]

Sometimes the discovery of a form brings with it the discovery of a whole method of speech, even a way of organizing a theme. There is a Welsh poem of the fourteenth century called *Englynion Y Clyweit*. It consists of a series of seven-syllable triplets in each one of which the question is asked, 'Did you hear what X said' and then, in the second line X is briefly described. The third line consists of an aphorism or proverb supposedly made by X and appropriate to his or her character. The form was essentially constructed as a means of remembering and gathering together proverbial statements. When I came across this *Englynion Y Clyweit* (the Welsh means simply 'Stanzas of Hearing') it struck me that the form and the method could be used again, and so I constructed a poem which I called, because it is really an imitation, *Englynion Y Clyweit*.

Lover, have you learned to hear,
whispered in the secret ear,
Love is all that love should fear ?

Have you heard the blackbird sing,
lifting up its burnished wing,
Love is darkness quarrelling ?

Have you listened to the sound
of the night owl on its round,
Love is what the vole has found ?

Have you heard at end of night
rafters creakingly recite,
Love is burdened by the light ?

[1] Rolfe Humphries, *Collected Poems*. Indiana University Press 1965, pp. 203–204.

Have you woken to the spell
rising from the moss-coped well,
Love is Heaven kissing Hell ?

Have you turned your head to hear
from the grasses on the weir,
Love is far, but Death is near ?

Has the sudden trodden stone
greeted you with helpless moan,
Love must mourn and lie alone ?

Have you heard the plover cry
from the ploughland to the sky,
Love is cloud run careless by ?

Have you listened to the snail
chaining leaf with silver trail,
Love is beak and Love is nail ?

Have you, tossing in your sheet,
heard the whisper at your feet,
Love is but a garnished meat ?

Have you heard within the wave
rearing from the seaman's grave,
Love will drown what Love would save ?

Yet, for all this, have you heard
with each dark and warning word,
Love is what God's finger stirred ?[1]

It is obvious that to appreciate this kind of poem fully the reader should
have some understanding of what precisely the poet has been up to, and
there are, I am afraid, only a very small number of readers fully able to
appreciate the skills of verse craft and the subtleties of poetic structure ;
as a consequence of this, a number of poets have gone so far as to maintain that they have ceased troubling themselves about the general reader
but write only for other poets. They no longer expect anyone but
another poet to appreciate and understand what they have made. Some
other poets, however, are deeply concerned to write in such a way that
the reasonably literate and informed general reader will not be confused
by esoteric references or allusions to matters that are not commonly

[1] Robin Skelton, *Country Songs*. The Sceptre Press 1973, pp. 3–4.

known. Auden, speaking of his poem *A Change of Air*, said 'One of the problems in writing a parable is finding images which will be devoid of any too specific historical or geographical associations for the reader, but at the same time be concrete enough to hold his interest'.[1] William Empson solved the problem of ensuring that his readers saw what he was doing by furnishing his poems with explanatory notes. If we place one of Empson's poems alongside his notes to it we get an extreme example of the way in which poetry can, by the sophisticated use of skills of compression and ambiguity, become absolutely impenetrable to all but a minority of readers. The poem that illustrates this well is *Dissatisfaction with Metaphysics*.

> High over Mecca Allah's prophet's corpse
> (The empty focus opposite the sun)
> Receives homage, centre of the universe.
> How smooth his epicycles round him run,
> Whose hearth is cold, and all his wives undone.
>
> Two mirrors with infinity to dine
> Drink him below the table when they please.
> Adam and Eve breed still their dotted line,
> Repeated incest, a plain series.
> Their trick is all philosophers' disease.
>
> New safe straight lines are finite though unbounded,
> Old epicycles numberless in vain.
> Then deeper than e'er plummet, plummet sounded,
> Then corpses flew, when God flooded the plain.
> He promised Noah not to flood again.[2]

The note reads:

There was a myth that no element would receive Mahomet's body, so that it hung between them and would appear self-subsisting. The earth's orbit being an ellipse has two foci with the sun at one of them; one might have a complicated theory, entirely wrong, making the other focus the important one. I failed to make a pun on *focus* and its original sense *hearth*. Two mirrors have any number of reflections (the self-conscious mind); a dotted line is used for 'and so on'. The mind

[1] Anthony Ostroff (ed.), *The Contemporary Poet as Artist and Critic*. Little, Brown and Company 1964, p. 184.

[2] William Empson, *Collected Poems*. Chatto and Windus 1955, p. 96.

makes a system by inbreeding from a few fixed ideas. Prosper's book of magical knowledge was buried deeper than ever plummet sounded, and the depths of knowledge which had previously been sounded became deepest during the disaster of the Flood.[1]

I do not myself think this a particularly good poem, but it does clearly illustrate how a poet drawing deeply upon his memory bank may create work which few people may understand. It illustrates, too, the way in which poetic 'learning' may differ from non-poetic, in that here the poet has brought together allusions to myth, science, grammar, philosophy, and literature to synthesize a new 'reading' of experience. And, of course, it clearly shows the wide range of the poet's interests and his capacity to pick up and use 'trifles' which few but a poet would think worthy of serious consideration. This poem, too, however, brings up the question of the esoteric in poetry. Is it proper for a poet to write in such a way that he can only be appreciated by that small audience of people who share his particular intellectual background and understand his allusions ? Is it proper for a poet to demand that his readers have read *The Tempest*, or the *Buddhist Fire Sermon*, or the Egyptian *Book of the Dead* ? Is it proper for him to require the reader of his 'version' or 'imitation' of a poem by (let us say) Baudelaire to know the original and thus be able to see how his version relates to it in a fashion which provides additional nuances and meanings ?

Each poet has to provide his own answer to these questions. Some, like Eliot, Pound, Empson, and occasionally Auden, have chosen to make considerable demands upon their readers. Some, like Blake, have required their readers to be familiar with a whole system of symbolism and philosophy which they have nowhere explained. Others, like Robert Graves and Yeats, have chosen to write books in which they have outlined the system of symbols and the philosophy which underlies and underpins their work. Even if a poet is not inclined towards the esoteric or the intellectually elaborate, however, he is aware that few of his readers will understand his work more than superficially. Poetry to the poet is 'a learned difficult art'; the majority of readers, however, like to regard it as little more than a way of expressing emotions and beliefs in memorable language. Jack Gilbert has expressed the poet's frustration in a poem he calls

[1] ibid., p. 95.

112

Orpheus in Greenwich Village

> What if Orpheus,
> confident in the hard-
> found mastery,
> should go down into Hell?
> Out of the clean light down?
> and then surrounded
> by the closing beasts
> and readying his lyre,
> should notice, suddenly,
> they had no ears?[1]

Poets who have, by long years of study and practice, developed that hard-found mastery to which Gilbert refers are keenly aware that their 'poetic scholarship' and their craftsmanship are rarely recognized even by that small number of critics who are so-called specialists in the field of contemporary poetry. Most full-length books of criticisms are devoted to a small number of major figures. In the twentieth century there have been countless critical examinations of W. B. Yeats, T. S. Eliot, and Ezra Pound, and a smaller number of books about Theodore Roethke, Robert Graves, W. H. Auden, Louis MacNiece, William Carlos Williams, Dylan Thomas, Robert Lowell, and Sylvia Plath. Of these eleven poets only two are still alive. Shorter critical studies of other poets have been published in various pamphlet series but most of these do little more than provide introductory essays which may be of use to students. There is, so far as I am aware, no full-length study of the poetry of David Jones, George Barker, Kathleen Raine, Edwin Muir, Randall Jarrell, W. S. Graham, Anthony Hecht, William Stafford, Richard Wilbur, John Heath-Stubbs, David Gascoyne, H. D., Vernon Watkins, James Dickey, A. R. Ammons, Stanley Kunitz, or Robert Penn Warren, to mention but a few of the poets whose work demands serious and thorough scrutiny, and even of these poets three are already dead.

The pursuit of poetry is, from this point of view, less than rewarding. Only a very small number of us will ever be able to feel that our work has been read carefully, that our craftsmanship has been appreciated, and that our messages have been understood. Many poets, finding that their confidence in their work suffers because they have no certainty of it ever being read, now have taken to giving more and more public readings of their poems. In this way they give themselves some assurance that an

---

[1] Jack Gilbert, *Views of Jeopardy*. Yale University Press 1962.

audience for their work actually exists, and they are able, in their commentary upon their poems, to direct the listener's attention to what they consider important or particularly interesting. This is not a completely satisfactory solution to the problem; it does however a little mitigate that intense feeling of futility which attacks those poets who pause to contemplate the years of work, the 'hard-found mastery' and, chillingly, suspect that nothing they have done has been of significance to any but a tiny group of fellow-poets and friends.

SIX Poems in their Beginnings

The exact combination of personal experience, cunning craftsmanship, poetic scholarship, and sheer luck which goes into the making of any one poem is hard to determine. Even the poet himself may not know exactly how he has managed to put the poem together. Nevertheless it is possible, by looking at the poets' accounts of the making of their poems, to see something of the way in which the memory bank is drawn upon and the verse-craft utilized. Let us first of all look at William Jay Smith's account of his writing the poem *Galileo Galilei*.

Galileo Galilei

Comes to knock and knock again
At a small secluded doorway
In the ordinary brain.

Into light the world is turning,
And the clocks are set for six;
And the chimney pots are smoking,
And the golden candlesticks.

Apple trees are bent and breaking,
And the heat is not the sun's;
And the Minotaur is waking,
And the streets are cattle runs.

Galileo Galilei,
In a flowing, scarlet robe,
While the stars go down the river
With the turning, turning globe,

Kneels before a black Madonna
And the angels cluster round
With grave, uplifted faces
Which reflect the shaken ground

And the orchard which is burning,
And the hills which take the light;
And the candles which have melted
On the altars of the night.

> Galileo Galilei
> Comes to knock and knock again
> At a small secluded doorway
> In the ordinary brain.

In Oxford in 1947 an acquaintance of mine told me one morning that he had awoken the previous night and found that the peculiar happenings of his dream had suggested to him the lines of a poem. He began to write them down, but he could not get beyond the opening:

> Galileo Galilei
> Comes to knock and knock again
> At a small secluded doorway
> In the ordinary brain.

I noted the lines down, and forgot about them until that same night when I found myself unable to sleep. I got up and wrote the poem down more or less as it now appears.

This may all sound suspect—à la 'Kubla Khan'—but it did really happen. The lines I now realize appealed to me particularly because I had just returned from my first trip to Florence, where I had been staying with friends in Pian dei Giullari, just around the corner from the house in which Galileo was living when Milton came to visit him. I was aware in writing the poem of many impressions of Italy, and of the movement of a kind of *mandala*, the dance of a priest around the altar.

In any case, I was rather pleased with what I had done and showed the result the next morning to my friend. He said indignantly that what I had written had nothing whatever to do with what he had had in mind. *Tant pis*, I replied, then he could certainly not expect to get credit for the lines. He agreed that they were now mine; and we have not met since.

Oddly enough, those readers who have admired the poem have all commented on its strange dreamlike quality.

William Jay Smith[1]

Here we see the combination of lucky chance with recent personal experience. John Wain gives us what he calls 'a clear (though not a complete) account' of the genesis of one of his poems, in which, again, sheer chance seems to have played a part, and in which his poetic scholarship led him to allude, though only in a prefatory quotation, to Euripides:

---

[1] Joseph Langland, op. cit., pp. 168–170.

Poem

HIPPOLYTUS: Do you see my plight, Queen, stricken as I am?
ARTEMIS: I see. But my eyes are not permitted to shed tears.
—Euripides, *Hippolytus*, 1395–96

Like a deaf man meshed in his endless silence
the earth goes swishing through the heavens' wideness.

Doubtless some god with benign inquiring brow
could lean over and let his brown eye so true

play over its whirling scabby hide with a look of searching
till suddenly, with eye and bland forefinger converging

he points to a specially found spot. *Here, this moment*
he might say, *I detect it; this is the locus of torment*:

This spot is the saddest on the earth's entire crust.
A quaint fancy? Such gods can scarcely exist?

Still, the fact outlives the metaphor it breeds;
whether or not the god exists, the scored earth bleeds.

There must be a point where pain takes its worst hold.
One spot, somewhere, holds the worst grief in the world.

Who would venture a guess as to where this grief lies cupped?
Ah, from minute to minute it could never be mapped.

For trouble flies between molecules like a dream.
It flowers from the snapped edge of bones like sour flame.

Who knows what child lies in a night like a mine-shaft
unblinking, his world like a fallen apple mashed and cleft?

Or what failed saint plummets into his private chasm
having bartered all Heaven for one stifling orgasm?

Or perhaps it is even an animal who suffers worst,
gentle furry bundle or two-headed obscene pest.

But where pain's purest drop burns deep no one could say,
unless it were this god with benign brown eye.

Some would curse this god for doing nothing to help.
But he has knowledge like cold water on his scalp.

To perceive that spirit of suffering in its raging purity
is to a god the burden of his divinity.

O then, if he exists, have pity on this god.
He is clamped to that wounded crust with its slime of blood.

He has no ignorance to hold him separate.
Everything is known to a god. The gods are desperate.

One evening in 1957 I was sitting alone in my flat, reading a news-paper, when I came upon a short news item, down at the bottom of a column, that seemed to me infinitely pathetic. I have forgotten the exact wording and most of the details, but the gist of it was that a small group of Italian soldiers, a dozen or so, had, by some strange quirk of military history, been taken prisoner by the Russians during the Second World War. None of these men had ever been heard of again, but one day—and this was the occasion of the news paragraph I was reading—a pigeon had been brought down, somewhere or other, with a piece of paper tied to its leg, bearing the desperate scrawled message that these Italians were engaged in slave labour somewhere in the Arctic Circle, and had been ever since 1945, and that they appealed to whoever found the pigeon's note to try to do something for them.

Sitting by my electric fire, the newspaper in my hand, I tried to put myself, imaginatively, in the place of these captives. But to be in their place, even imaginatively, was so horrible that I soon gave it up, and my mind turned, almost with relief, to thinking along more general lines. The sheer concentration of human misery in the hut where the Italians were kept: the desperate whispered conversations; the incredible patience that must have gone into snaring the pigeon and managing to get it away with the note tied to its leg, without being seen by the guards; their emotions as the bird flew away out of sight; finally, the numbing certainty that nothing could be done for them. Their crime, which was simply to be conscripted into the army of their country, was to be punished without end; nothing lay before them but misery and death. I tried to image a suffering worse than theirs: if I couldn't, did this mean that the spot which contained them was the unhappiest spot on the earth's surface? Then the thought broke in on me that, quite probably, the deepest and most inconsolable grief in the world, if one could know where it was, might have nothing to do with political persecution, slavery or any cruelty inflicted from outside. At this thought, the poem began to move inside me, and within half an hour I had it written in the form in which it is printed here. The epigraph from Euripedes was added later, when it became plain that the poem had naturally moved, or wandered, towards the subject of a possible divinity and its nature.

JOHN WAIN[1]

[1] ibid., pp. 230–231 and pp. 232–233.

Barbara Howes reveals the way in which knowledge of verse-craft is brought to bear not only upon the form but also upon the whole thematic viewpoint of a poem. She writes:

> *Mirror Image: Port-au-Prince*
> *Au petit*
> *Salon de Coiffeur*
> Monique's / hands fork
> like lightning, like a baton
> rise / to lead her client's hair
> *in repassage*: she irons out the kinks.
> Madame's brown cheek / is dusted over with a
> paler shade / of costly powder. Nails and lips are red.
>
> Her matching lips and nails incarnadined, / in the
> next booth Madam consults her face / imprisoned
> in the glass. Her lovely tan / is almost
> gone. Oh, watch Yvonne's astute
> conductor fingers set the
> permanent, / *In little*
> *Drawing-room of*
> *Hairdresser!*

This poem derived from a number of impressions gathered during our four-month sojourn in the town of Pétionville, three or four miles up the road from the capital city of Haiti in the West Indies. I had occasion, of course, to go to the hairdresser, and could not help but notice that the process took rather longer than it does at home; and this was due quite simply to the fact that the operator had to go against her usual practice by trying to insert some curl into my straight locks, while ordinarily she used her skill to smooth them out. I felt rather keenly the ironies of life on noticing this, and then for some reason recalled pictures I used to draw again and again as a child. One 'sameby' was a rabbit: long ears, short tail, a jacket and tie and belt. The other 'sameby,' a squirrel: short ears, bushy long tail, jacket, belt, and tie. Well, thinking of my interest in a good wave and a proper tan, I found myself playing further with the idea and felt that there must be a poem somewhere in this subject for me. On the way up by bus to our house, there was a sign tacked to a tree with the words: '*Au petit salon de coiffeur.*' I had a starting point.

It then came to me that the question of the form of this poem would be important and I suddenly saw how form in this special case could be employed in the aid of meaning. I arranged the poem on the page so that it looks like two triangles, the bottom one pointing downward; the whole is thus shaped like a diamond, with a space cutting it in half. The mirror is the line drawn between the two verses, but perhaps really it is not a mirror at all, but a piece of glass, and the two female figures sitting there on each side look through it, and believe that the other's state is more desirable. It is perfection that one wants to see in a mirror: but life does not always allow this.[1]

Sometimes a complete poem may emerge from a problem of verse itself. I have always been interested in various kinds of repetition in poetry. I am fascinated particularly by the use of rime riche, where the two rhyming words are spelt exactly the same way but may carry slightly different meanings. I'm also fascinated by verse forms such as the Sestina and the Canzone in which a small number of words are repeated over and over again in a set pattern at the ends of the lines of each stanza. It occurred to me that it might be possible to make a poem in which, with a couple of exceptions to avoid monotony, the end-word of the first line would be the same as that of the second line, the third line would have the same end-word as the fourth, and so on, relaxing the rule only for the last two lines in all but the last stanza, thus providing a certain fluidity. I felt, too, that the poem should have a touch of rhyme about it—not too much or it might become stilted or too ostentatiously ingenious. Having thought of this I tried to work out an opening. I thought that if the poem were going to be constructed around obsessive repetition the speaker of it should reveal his anxiety from the beginning. What sort of anxiety could set him to puzzling? The word *reason* came to mind immediately as one way of getting at that ever-recurring *Why* with which children attack their parents and men and women attack each other. The problem, I felt, must be presented as insoluble. The poem that emerged, with a kind of measured inevitability, is one I call *No Appeal*, and, as it neared its conclusion I realized that I could make it even more obsessive and anxious, if at the very end the speaker returned to his original question, only altering it slightly so as to make it sound a little more desperate.

> Is there a reason?
> Can there be a reason?
> She turns away
> as if there were no way
> for me to make amends.
> But what amends?
> And for what sin—
> omission or commission?

[1] Howard Nemerov (ed.), *Poets on Poetry*. Basic Books 1966, pp. 64–65.

How can I know?
If asked, she'll say 'You know,
And you know very well!'
and tears will well
in those hurt eyes
as, wonderingly, she eyes
the sudden stranger
that once fooled her so

with love's high vision,
and betrays that vision
with his question.
Love would never question
Love-decided guilt
but would plead guilt.
Is there no reason?
Can there be no reason?

This poem of mine is, perhaps, only a little more than mere verse-craft. Richard Eberhardt's account of his writing of *New Hampshire, February* shows another aspect of the poet's memory bank, for he could not, it seems have made his poem had he not read Schopenhauer and Thomas Hardy, and a key image is that of Michelangelo's painting of God creating Adam.

Here is 'New Hampshire, February,' a poem dating from the end of the 1930's. I was as yet unmarried and had been given a cabin in Kensington, New Hampshire, near Exeter, during the winter vacation. The only heat was from the kitchen stove. I read philosophy and wrote poetry. One day some wasps fell through the roof onto the stove. They were numb but moved toward the center, getting more lively all the time. Recognizing a threat, I pushed them to the outside where they grew slower immediately. I first did this innocently, by instinct. However, I had early read much Schopenhauer and Hardy and soon decided to play with these creatures as the instrument of their fate, 'malice prepense'. I would push them toward the center of the stove. They would become lively, buzzing their wings, able to sting. Then I would immediately move them toward the outer edge of the stove where they would quickly become gelid. I manipulated them at will. The philosophical implications of this in the relation of ourselves to God were immediately to hand and I wrote the following poem, with changes from the above facts which you will see. For instance, I use my breath instead of my hands as agent. There is an allusion to and reminder of 'God touching his finger to Adam' from Michelangelo's Sistine painting.

New Hampshire, February

Nature has made them hide in crevices,
Two wasps so cold they looked like bark.
Why I do not know, but I took them
And I put them
In a metal pan, both day and dark.

Like God touching his finger to Adam
I felt, and thought of Michelangelo,
For whenever I breathed on them,
The slightest breath,
They leaped, and preened as if to go.

My breath controlled them always quite.
More sensitive than electric sparks
They came into life
Or they withdrew to ice,
While I watched, suspending remarks.

Then one in a blind career got out,
And fell to the kitchen floor, I
Crushed him with my cold ski boot,
By accident. The other
Had not the wit to try or die.

And so the other is still my pet.
The moral of this is plain.
But I will shirk it.
You will not like it. And
God does not live to explain.[1]

Eberhardt's account reveals clearly the way in which a poet's reading of philosophy can make him aware of ways in which a simple experience can be made to illuminate and even embody a profound vision of the human predicament. Robert Lowell, writing of his poem *Skunk Hour* also reveals a well-stocked memory bank, and shows how a poet may bring into juxtaposition images and experiences which none but a poet would think of yoking together.

Skunk Hour
(for Elizabeth Bishop)

Nautilus Island's hermit
heiress still lives through winter in her Spartan cottage;
her sheep still graze above the sea.

[1] ibid., pp. 25–26.

Her son's a bishop. Her farmer
is first selectman in our village;
she's in her dotage.

Thirsting for
the hierarchic privacy
of Queen Victoria's century,
she buys up all
the eyesores facing her shore,
and lets them fall.

The season's ill—
we've lost our summer millionaire,
who seemed to leap from an L.L. Bean
catalogue. His nine-knot yawl
was auctioned off to lobstermen.
A red fox stain covers Blue Hill.

And now our fairy
decorator brightens his shop for fall;
his fishnet's filled with orange cork,
orange, his cobbler's bench and awl;
there is no money in his work,
he'd rather marry.

One dark night,
my Tudor Ford climbed the hill's skull;
I watched for love-cars. Lights turned down,
they lay together, hull to hull,
where the graveyard shelves on the town . . .
My mind's not right.

A car radio bleats,
'Love, O careless Love . . .' I hear
my ill-spirit sob in each blood cell,
as if my hand were at its throat. . . .
I myself am hell;
nobody's here——

only skunks, that search
in the moonlight for a bite to eat.
They march on their soles up Main Street:
white stripes, moonstruck eyes' red fire
under the chalk-dry and spar spire
of the Trinitarian Church.

I stand on top
of our back steps and breathe the rich air—
a mother skunk with her column of kittens swills the garbage pail.
She jabs her wedge-head in a cup
of sour cream, drops her ostrich tail,
and will not scare.

What I can describe and what no one else can describe are the circumstances of my poem's composition. I shan't reveal private secrets.
. . . 'Skunk Hour' was begun in mid-August, 1957, and finished about a month later. In March of the same year, I had been giving readings on the West Coast, often reading six days a week and sometimes twice on a single day. I was in San Francisco, the era and setting of Allen Ginsberg, and all about very modest poets were waking up prophets. I became sorely aware of how few poems I had written, and that these few had been finished at the latest three or four years earlier. Their style seemed distant, symbol-ridden and wilfully difficult. I began to paraphrase my Latin quotations, and to add extra syllables to a line to make it clearer and more colloquial. I felt my old poems hid what they were really about, and many times offered a stiff, humorless and even impenetrable surface. I am no convert to the 'beats'. I know too well that the best poems are not necessarily poems that read aloud. Many of the greatest poems can only be read to one's self, for inspiration is no substitute for humor, shock, narrative and a hypnotic voice, the four musts for oral performance. Still, my own poems seemed like prehistoric monsters dragged down into the bog and death by their ponderous armor. I was reciting what I no longer felt. What influenced me more than San Francisco and reading aloud was that for some time I had been writing prose. I felt that the best style for poetry was none of the many poetic styles in English, but something like the prose of Chekhov or Flaubert.

When I returned to my home I began writing lines in a new style. No poem, however, got finished and soon I left off and tried to forget the whole headache. Suddenly, in August, I was struck by the sadness of writing nothing, and having nothing to write, of having, at least, no language. When I began writing 'Skunk Hour', I felt that most of what I knew about writing was a hindrance.

The dedication is to Elizabeth Bishop, because re-reading her suggested a way of breaking through the shell of my old manner. Her rhythms, idiom, images, and stanza structure seemed to belong to a later century. 'Skunk Hour' is modeled on Miss Bishop's 'The Armadillo,' a much better poem and one I had heard her read and had later carried around with me. Both 'Skunk Hour' and 'The

Armadillo' use short line stanzas, start with drifting description and end with a single animal.

This was the main source. My others were Hölderlin's '*Brod und Wein*,' particularly the moon lines:

Sieh! und das Schattenbild unserer Erde, der Mond,
kommet geheim nun auch; die Schwärmerische, die Nacht kommt
wohl mit Sternen und wohl wenig bekummert um uns,

and so forth. I put this in long straggling lines and then added touches of Maine scenery, till I saw I was getting nowhere. Another source, probably undetectable now, was Annette von Droste-Hülshoff's 'Am letzten Tage des Jahres'. She too uses a six-line stanza with short lines. Her second stanza is as follows:

's ist tiefe Nacht!
Ob wohl ein Auge offen noch?
In diesen Mauern ruttelt dein
Verrinnen, Zeit! Mir schaudert; doch
Es will die letzte Stunde sein
Einscarn durchwacht.

Geschehen all

Here and elsewhere, my poem and the German poem have the same shudders and situation.

'Skunk Hour' was written backwards, first the last two stanzas, I think, and then the next to last two. Anyway, there was a time when I had the last four stanzas much as they now are and nothing before them. I found the bleak personal violence repellent. All was too close, though watching the lovers was not mine, but from an anecdote about Walt Whitman in his old age. I began to feel that real poetry came, not from fierce confessions, but from something almost meaningless but imagined. I was haunted by an image of a blue china doorknob. I never used the doorknob, or knew what it meant, yet somehow it started the current of images in my opening stanzas. They were written in reverse order, and at last gave my poem an earth to stand on, and space to breathe.[1]

The same capacity for yoking together ideas and images is revealed by Tony Connor in his discussion of *Hill-Top and Guy Fawkes*. Connor also shows clearly how actual and imaginative experience relate to each other. The account is taken from a tape recording Tony Connor made to be played to students.

[1] Anthony Ostroff, op. cit., pp. 82–83 and pp. 108–110.

I should perhaps tell you that in the North of England a small reservoir serving a mill—probably a Victorian Cotton Mill or Bleach or Dye Works—is called a 'lodge'.

Hill-Top and Guy Fawkes

Not more than his nose and one eye
was showing. He lurked, as though shy
of being caught looking—like an elderly spinster
behind her curtains when a wedding goes by.

Before we saw him seemed like an age
of fishing become shove and nudge;
one of the boys shouted, and there he was poking
slyly dead through the looped-back scum on the lodge.

The police came with iron hooks.
They shooed us off. We made tracks.
behind the rusting dump of machinery
and, still as cogs among the little hillocks

of clinker, watched while they dragged him out.
The newspaper said he was seventy-eight,
'of no fixed abode': we played at being vagrants
the rest of the summer holidays, hobbling about

with sacking on our feet, and caps
held out for pennies. Then the shops
began to sell fireworks, and in our fathers cellars
we laboured to build the burnable human shapes.[1]

The ambiguity in question is the possessive 'fathers' in the final verse. Is it singular or plural? To explain the use of it I must go right back to the beginning of the poem. In fact as the origin of this poem is neatly explicable I shall utilize this rare opportunity and tell you how the poem first started in my mind. I worked twelve miles from the large industrial city in which I was born and every day for three years I travelled by diesel train along the man-made squalor of the once pleasant Vale of Irwell. Every day I passed the same lodge with the same scum blown back (by the prevailing wind I suppose) to reveal about half the water's brightness. 'It is like a lace curtain looped back from a shining window', I thought one day in summer. In Autumn I imagined a corpse floating in the water under the scum which I'd already given a name to. It would inevitably be a secretive person peeping forth. 'Who peeps from behind the curtains?' I asked myself.

[1] Tony Connor, *Lodgers*. Oxford University Press 1965, p. 42.

Why, elderly spinsters ! 'What at ?' Well, things they regret having missed, though they won't admit it. 'Such as ?' Weddings, I suppose. 'Is it a spinster, then, in the lodge ?' In a way, yes. It's a vagrant, a man who's missed out—unaccommodated man, without a home, without a family. 'Well, to sustain the analogy, what will he be peeping secretly at ?' Children enjoying themselves, what else ! By winter—these decisions and ruminations were all very slow—I had remembered the occasion in my childhood when I was indeed present at the dredging of a corpse from a lodge. I knew, simultaneously, that I was making the whole thing up, but the 'memory' was very vivid. It all happened in one of the very few undeveloped areas in our locality— a place called Hill Top. Now it looked as if it was going to be a poem about childhood—childhood and death—but I wasn't clear about anything except the incident of the sighting of the corpse. By this time I was down to the end of the second verse and the law entered naturally, the adult system impinging upon and almost overpowering the vision of children. 'Still as cogs' was a happy simile. Nothing is less still than cogs in use; therefore nothing is stiller than cogs on a rusting dump. The end of the poem arrived as a complete surprise and seemed to possess that autonomous presence that makes one believe—as Coleridge or somebody else that's dead said—that one is merely the midwife at the birth. The playing at vagrants had to take place in the summer holidays, and after that the next big date in the child's year is Bonfire Night when the effigy of Guy Fawkes is burned. Children playing with death, and then the accurate description of the way in which we built the effigies of Guy Fawkes in the cellars of our houses, out of the way. I remember going down and being frightened (even though I was expecting it) by the giant-sized doll made from old clothes stuffed with newspapers that lolled in one corner amidst the cobwebs. Yet the ear accepts 'our fathers' cellars' in the sense of 'our Father who art in heaven' and the cellars become Hell or the human subconscious in which we labour to build the 'burnable human shapes'—not 'inflammable', which *might* burn, but 'burnable' which are intended for burning, acceptable offerings to placate the monster that lusts for us all—Guy Fawkes or the anonymous animals in Auschwitz. The poem, which followed a well-lit if crooked road, suddenly lunges into the dark wood which, almost unnoticed, had been blocking the view on one side since we began.

Of course none of these accounts is complete, as John Wain admits of his own. One cannot ever describe the genesis of a poem with absolute certainty that one has missed nothing out, and one may well find oneself unintentionally rationalizing an intuitive process in order to make clear what, in reality, has always been, and will remain, obscure. Barbara Howes makes the point well:

> The whole question of the origin of a poem is of course a large and a vague one. Who can tell ? Who knows what trivial impression, stored up for years, may not suddenly, on coming up against some new impression, suddenly produce an image, an idea, a poem ? But to be overprecise about what may have brought about a poem would be foolhardy. For after all, no poet is completely in the know about the source of his work, or even how he may have managed to improve it. He sees certain things, he cuts what is clearly bad and tries to repair the weak points, but he can hardly pretend to complete critical good sense, quite simply because no one has it.[1]

Barbara Howes' statement is particularly true, of course, of the totally 'inspired' poem which arrives as if dictated by someone else, the poet being himself only aware, as he writes, that the words are coming one after the other, and appear to be getting somewhere. The most famous of these completely 'inspired' poems is Coleridge's *Kubla Khan*, and Livingston Lowes has shown in his book, *The Road to Xanadu*, that, in making this poem, though entranced at the time, Coleridge drew upon a memory bank of enormous proportions, bringing together information and images from a huge number of books. It is clear, indeed, that the poet must have a well-stocked mind so that he can, when the creative impulse is upon him, either consciously or intuitively, make use of a great deal of material. The learning, the scholarship of the poem may not be the same as that of the historian or critic, but it is nevertheless a real scholarship, even though the poet himself may not realize, until the poem arrives, the full extent of his experience and knowledge.

[1] Howard Nemerov, op. cit., p. 64.

SEVEN The Many Modern Modes

In the last chapter I attempted to show the different ways in which poets find themselves combining personal experience, scholarship, and sheer chance in the making of their poems, and also showed how the poets used the association of ideas to develop their themes in effective but surprising directions. A poet's studies, however, do not lead him only into the reading of a great many books of history, philosophy, and whatever other subjects fascinate him, as well as into the garnering and recalling of personal experience. They also lead him into a highly sophisticated examination of techniques. The poet reads other poems not only because he derives pleasure from reading them, but also in order to learn from them, as Blake learned from Ossian, Coleridge from Bowles, Pope from Dryden, Eliot from Laforgue, Pound from Whitman, Auden from Byron, and Robert Creeley from William Carlos Williams. Sometimes it is easy to see exactly what one poet has learned from another; sometimes only the poet can tell us that a particular way of speech, a certain construction, is one he owes to his study of somebody else's technique. In the twentieth century there has been so great an amount of innovation that the poet of today is embarrassed by the number of technical devices being practised by living writers. There are now not three or four main styles of composition, as in the eighteenth and seventeenth centuries, but scores. Moreover, almost every poet of stature in the last fifty years has contributed a new poetic device to the existing stock.

It is obviously impossible to list all the discoveries made by the poets in the last fifty years. It is possible to look at a few of them, however, and show the way in which the poet's scrutiny of contemporary work differs from that of the ordinary reader and the usual kind of literary critic. The poet, in reading a given poem, is usually less concerned to interpret its 'meaning', to evaluate its significance and to see it in its historical context, than he is to spot some device that he himself may be able to use, or to develop, for his own purposes. Consequently, while the academic critic concentrates upon (let us say) the 'message' of Auden's *Age of Anxiety* and only comments in passing upon Auden's use

129

of Anglo-Saxon alliterative verse, the poet is likely to concentrate upon the way the verse itself is constructed, and to consider whether or not it works as a medium of expression. The poet will observe that Yeats used the word *that* in a highly idiosyncratic fashion for particular purposes, though he may not be greatly troubled as to the exact significance of the word *gyre* unless he is also interested, coincidentally, in Yeats as a visionary and thinker as well as a poet. He will be more interested in those poems of Robert Francis which have the same number of words in each line than in Francis's other poems. He will scrutinize Austin Clarke's use of rime riche rather than devote himself wholeheartedly to what the poems are about.

Here I am exaggerating a little, for poets are also close readers of poetry and as likely as anyone else to be excited by the messages of poems and their emotional power. It is perhaps a matter of priorities. I admit, freely, that my first reading of any poem is always a scanning of it for matters of technical interest. I 'read' the poem, I might say, at the second reading. This scanning process can perhaps best be illustrated by taking a number of poems of different kinds and showing what is technically significant about them. Consider Louis MacNeice's poem, *The Sunlight on the Garden*. The first verse sets the pattern for all the four stanzas.

> The sunlight on the garden
> Hardens and grows cold,
> We cannot cage the minute
> Within its nets of gold
> When all is told,
> We cannot beg for pardon.[1]

The cunning of this stanza fascinates me. The last two syllables of the first and third lines rhyme with the first two syllables of the second and fourth lines. The end rhymes run abcbba, but the c line is similar to the a lines in ending with an unstressed syllable, while the other lines end with stressed ones. Moreover the 'c' and 'g' and 't' sounds make up a pattern of their own thus:

> Line 1 : t and g
> Line 2 : g and c
> Line 3 : 2c and 2t and soft g
> Line 4 : 2t and g
> Line 5 : t
> Line 6 : c and g

[1] E. R. Dodds (ed.), *The Collected Poems of Louis MacNeice*. Faber 1966, p. 84.

If we listen carefully to the sound we notice, too, that the hard 'g' and hard 'c' sounds are similar to each other and only differ by being made at different places in the mouth; they are, indeed, both voiced velar plosive consonants. The 'd' and 't' sounds have the same relationship, both being alveolar plosive consonants. Moreover, every line contains an 'n' sound and four of them contain two. The same sort of consonantal pattern runs through the whole poem.

Contemplating this craftsmanship I find myself saying, 'What can I learn from this?' The answer is that 'It is possible to construct a lyrical stanza in terms of a deliberately limited set of consonants, and to emphasize the musical nature of the stanza by adding internal disyllabic rhyme.' Having spotted this my natural tendency is to try and do it, without appearing to actually imitate MacNeice's poem. It is clear that if disyllabic internal rhyme is to be used I cannot have a very short line or too much space will be taken up by the rhyming syllables. I must, therefore, have a six-syllable line at the very least. MacNeice's lines run in numbers of syllables 7, 5, 7, 6, 4, 7. Perhaps, in order to avoid using his tune, I should try for something like 8 syllables, and sometimes have either 7 or 9.

> Alone in quiet wandering,
> daring to clear my mind,
> of all unclear and sundering,
> adoring life and wind, . . .

It might take several hours from this unpromising beginning to work out how I could use my discovery, or, indeed, if I am able to use it to produce anything but an exercise, but at the end of it all, I will have added another technical implement to my tool-kit.

It may be the metre or rhyme which I am attracted by when I read a poem that I feel may teach me something. It may just as frequently be an over-all method of approach. Consider Ted Hughes' poem, *Crow's Song of Himself.*

> When God hammered Crow
> He made gold
> When God roasted Crow in the sun
> He made diamond
> When God crushed Crow under weights
> He made alcohol
> When God tore Crow to pieces
> He made money

When God blew Crow up
He made day
When God hung Crow on a tree
He made fruit
When God buried Crow in the earth
He made man
When God tried to chop Crow in two
He made woman
When God said: 'You win, Crow,'
He made the Redeemer.

When God went off in despair
Crow stopped his beak and started in on the two thieves.[1]

This poem is, perhaps, not absolutely successful, for it is difficult to see
the connection between cause and effect as being anything but arbitrary.
The poem asserts as a myth asserts, but, unlike a myth, it does not lead
to anything but an enigma. Nevertheless the structure is interesting.
Can I use cause and effect in this fashion, piling mystery upon mystery,
and assertion upon assertion, without stealing too obviously from
Hughes (though Hughes himself took the poetic formula from hints in
tribal chants and ancient spells and charms)?

Before you touched my hand,
I was dust on a stone

Before you smiled at me
I was withered grass

Before your mouth met mine
I was broken twigs

Who now, as I hear your name,
am a shuddering forest.

This is, again, only a draft to work on. It lacks 'punch' and is self-
indulgently sentimental, even narcissistic. Hughes' poem, however,
points the way for me to investigate other poems that derive from
ancient and magical formulae, and I remember chants and spells by
other poets that I should now look up in order to explore the technique
further.

Sometimes a poet is interested, not in a complete poem, but in a few
lines which contain a particular device. Theodore Roethke has, in

[1] Ted Hughes, *Crow*. Faber 1970, p. 61.

several poems, made use of the child's viewpoint. He has, in simple declarative sentences, tried to mimic both the sensuality and the unconnected quality of infant experience. In *Where Knock Is Open Wide* he wrote

> A kitten can
> Bite with his feet;
> Papa and Mama
> Have more teeth.
>
> Sit and Play
> Under the rocker
>   Until the cows
>   All have puppies.
> His ears haven't time.
> Sing me a sleep-song please.
> A real hurt is soft.[1]

In *I Need, I Need,* he wrote

> A deep dish. Lumps in it.
> I can't taste my mother.
> Hoo. I know the spoon
> Sit in my mouth.
>
> A sneeze can't sleep.
> Diddle we care
> Couldly.[2]

It is hard to see how one could use this particular method without attempting like Roethke, to speak from a child's viewpoint. It is not, however, impossible. There are states of mind and situations which can only be presented accurately in terms of uncoordinated sensations and nonsense-phrases. Let us suppose the speaker of the poem is half asleep in bed in the early morning. His pillow is hard and he has a slight cramp in his foot.

> My ear stings.
> Rocks have pushy voices.
> Turn over to birds;
> They shout at the crab on my foot.
> I am not here, quite, yet.
> The wall is a ceiling.
> Who made this cave of wool?
> If I remember my name
> I will lose the island.

[1] *The Collected Poems of Theodore Roethke.* Doubleday 1966, p. 71.
[2] ibid., p. 74.

This sounds much too like Roethke to be at all useful. Clearly one cannot use the whole method, but only part of it. Let us attack the problem again, and alter the speaker's approach.

> Do you remember how?
> First light, then smell—
> bacon? Or still the horses in the dream?
> Morning must lock the horses up, of course?
> And I must lift my hurt head from the stones
> And call this courtyard bed,
> Which now it is,
> And cries of all the huntsmen
> morning birds.

What seems to be emerging now is a way of showing how the dream and the reality mingle at the point of waking, and how still uncoordinated sensations appear, for a little time, to relate to one another, one world fusing with another.

A good deal of twentieth-century poetry has been concerned to fuse past and present, dream and reality, in this way, and to suggest that what we dream or remember, however fleetingly, may somehow be as or more significant than the 'actual world'. One can see this in the shifting perspectives of T. S. Eliot's *The Waste Land* and *Four Quartets*, as well as in the so-called 'Confessional' poetry of Robert Lowell and Anne Sexton. Indeed the poetry of the twentieth century has gone some way towards reshaping the spoken dramatic monologue which is central to the work of Robert Browning and, later, Edward Thomas and Robert Frost, as an internal, half spoken, half-thought or dreamed monologue. The fusion of dream with memory, and the use of dream material in contemporary poetry, owes much to the Surrealist movement of course. André Breton, the main leader and spokesman for the movement defined *Surrealism* in 1924 as:

> Pure psychic automatism, by which it is intended to express, verbally, in writing, or by other means, the real process of thought. Thought's dictation, in the absence of all control exercised by the reason and outside all aesthetic or moral preoccupations.[1]

Not all Surrealist poetry was entirely automatic or the product of free association fantasies, though much of it was. The attempt was also deliberately, and consciously, to bring dream and fantasy back into

[1] Quoted in David Gascoyne, *A Short Survey of Surrealism*. Cobden-Sanderson 1936, p. 61. Translation by David Gascoyne.

poetry. Hugh Sykes Davies said 'Surrealism . . . has found itself faced by a violent divorce between the worlds of action and dream, reality and phantasy, and has protected against this divorce.'[1] George Hugnet describes Alfred Jarry's work as 'Obscure, with whimsicality and a passion for the terminology of heraldry, precious and scintillating, chaotic and full of wonders, his poems with their irreplaceable dream imagery, never beautiful, most admirable, are a key to a thrilling world seen through the magnifications and interpretations of the unconscious'.[2] Here is Alfred Jarry's poem, *Fable*, in A. L. Lloyd's translation.

A tin of corned beef, chained like a lorgnette
Saw a lobster go by, bearing a family resemblance to her.
He was buckled within a hard case
On which it was written that inside, like her, he was boneless
(Boneless and economical)
And beneath his folded tail,
He probably hid a key for opening her.
Lovestricken, the sedentary corned beef
Declared to the little automobile box of living preserves
That if he'd deign to acclimatise himself
Staying by her side, in the terrestrial shopfront,
He too would be decorated with many gold medals.

A.L.L.[3]

This is a fantastic anecdote, as are many poems of the surrealists. Many others take the form of catalogues. André Masson provides an excellent example while also commenting upon Surrealist methods, in his poem *Poetic Objectivity*. I give it in David Gascoyne's translation.

Poetic Objectivity

only exists in the succession, the linking together of all the subjective elements of which the poet, until the beginning of the new order, is not the master but the slave.

War of wanderers and guides
Contrary to apprehensions
Contrary to advice
Far from the most sensitive shores
To fly from the salubrious seas
Hope's early endeavours

[1] In Herbert Read (ed.), *Surrealism*. Faber 1936, p. 147.
[2] ibid., p. 201.
[3] In *Contemporary Poetry and Prose*, No. 2 1936, pp. 32–33.

> To fly from the inhuman colours
> Tempests with lifeless gestures
> And great empty bodies
> The labyrinth of exiled stars
> The oceans of milk and wine and meats
> The waves of fur and the waves of sleep
> The sand in its bed
> To fly from the ships and their appointed tasks.[1]

Surrealism was not particularly influential upon poetry written in English until relatively recently. Though some American and British poets were near-surrealists in the period 1935–1945, it was not until the sixties that a post-surrealist or neo-surrealist movement began in the United States, its main vehicle being the magazine *Kayak*. Now there is a great deal of surrealist and near-surrealist poetry being written. It rarely appears to be automatic; it does not restrict itself to fables and catalogues: it is, indeed, a much more versatile poetry than that of most of the first members of the movement. Here is an example by James Tate.

Exposition

> There was no line for the pavilion
> of emptiness. I walked right in.
> I admired the pure space and lack
>
> of sound; there were absolutely no
> movies, and I was asked to observe
> the invention of nothing carefully.
> My feet moved freely like dolphins
>
> in a gulf stream. O my sadness
> flew at the ceiling in a balloon
> of laughter. So many better men
> would have given their lives
>
> for this. Now the astonishing parabolas
> of desire are going, and my dangling
> hands melt onto a distant floor.[2]

Tate has learned from the early surrealists, and has developed a kind of metaphysical or philosophical poetry which uses dream images and bizarre juxtapositions in order to present states of mind which cannot be

---

[1] Alan Clodd and Robin Skelton (eds.), *David Gascoyne: Collected Verse Translations*. Oxford University Press 1970, p. 24.
[2] James Tate, *The Torches*. Unicorn Press 1968, p. (16).

presented rationally. He is not a pure surrealist. His work shows, however, how a poet can, by scrutinizing the technical devices of other poets,
learn to use them for his own purposes. Tate has, of course, learned a
method of approach as I attempted to do with Ted Hughes and Theodore Roethke, rather than a verbal device of the kind I tried to learn
from MacNeice.

There is almost no end to the process of learning the craft of poetry, if
one is truly concerned to develop one's capacities for exploration and
expression. Many poets, however, choose to stop short of trying all the
techniques that are displayed by twentieth-century poetry, and for a
good reason. The twentieth century has been, since the end of its first
decade, a period of intense experimentation and any poet who follows
up all the innovations of the period is likely to become nothing more
than a player of verbal games. Nevertheless no poet can afford to be
entirely unaware of the experiments that have been made, and especially
those which suggest radical new approaches to language.

e. e. cumming's poetry is particularly significant in this respect. His
inventiveness was such as to startle his first readers and bewilder conven-
tionally-minded publishers. He played tricks with typography and
spelling in an attempt to get closer both to actual speech and to an
accurate presentation of sensation. Thus, poem 19 of his 95 *Poems* reads:

> un(bee)mo
>
> vi
>
> n(in)g
> are(th
> e)you(o
> nly)
>
> asl(rose)eep[1]

This is an attempt to present two perceptions simultaneously. The words
outside the brackets read 'unmoving are you asleep'; the words inside
the brackets read 'bee in the only rose'. In another poem (poem 16 of
Xaipe)[2] in order to mimic the movement he described, he wrote

> The green robe
>
> o
>
> p
>
> e
>
> n
>
> s

[1] e. e. cummings, *Complete Poems*. MacGibbon and Kee 1968, Vol II, p. 691.
[2] ibid., p. 614.

The seventh poem of *One Times One*[1] begins

> ygUDuh
>
>> ydoan
>> yunnuhstan
>>
>> ydoan o
>> yunnuhstan dem
>> yguduh ged
>>
>> yunnuhstan dem doidee
>> yguduh ged riduh
>> ydoan o nudn
>
> LISN bud LISN
>
>>> dem
>>> gud
>>> am
>>>
>>> lidl yelluh bas
>>> tuds weer goin
>
> duhSIVILEYEzum

This is so spelt as to give the reader the exact accent of the speaker. An English 'translation' would read 'You got to! You don't (you understand) You don't know them! You got to get (you understand) them dirty—you got to get rid of—(you don't know nothing—Listen, bud, listen!)—them goddam little yellow bastards. We're going to civilize em!' Here the joke is that the illiterate speaker is betraying himself as ignorant by the way in which he speaks and yet expressing a desire to 'civilize' someone else.

e. e. cumming's technical tricks are numerous and so very individual and idiosyncratic that it is hard to make use of them oneself. Nevertheless, cumming's work does lead one to wonder if one cannot enliven ordinary speech in some way and perhaps make fuller use of parentheses, capitalization, and phonetic spelling, and of space.

Charles Olson in his influential essay on *Projective Verse* clearly showed how he, as a poet, learned from cummings' experiments. He suggested in this essay that poets should work in 'projective or OPEN verse'. He maintained in this essay that 'FORM IS NEVER MORE THAN AN EXTENSION OF CONTENT' and that 'ONE PERCEPTION MUST IMMEDIATELY AND DIRECTLY LEAD TO A FURTHER

---

[1] ibid., p. 547.

PERCEPTION' and emphasized the importance of paying attention to
the syllable, saying

> It would do no harm, as an act of correction to both prose and verse
> as now written, if both rime and meter, and, in the quantity words,
> both sense and sound, were less in the forefront of the mind than the
> syllable, if the syllable, that fine creature, were more allowed to lead
> the harmony on. With this warning, to those who would try: to step
> back here to this place of the elements and minims of language, is to
> engage speech where it is least careless—and least logical. Listening
> for the syllables must be so constant and so scrupulous, the exaction
> must be so complete, that the assurance of the ear is purchased at the
> highest—40 hours a day—price.[1]

To these contentions he adds a further one: that, in our time, we can be
assisted by the typewriter, for

> It is the advantage of the typewriter that, due to its rigidity and its
> space precisions, it can, for a poet, indicate exactly the breath, the
> pauses, the suspensions even of syllables, the juxtaposition even of
> parts of phrases, which he intends. For the first time the poet has the
> stave and the bar a musician has had. For the first time he can, without
> the convention of rime and meter, record the listening he has done to
> his own speech and by that one act indicate how he would want any
> reader, silently or otherwise, to voice his work.
>
> It is time we picked the fruits of the experiments of cummings,
> Pound, Williams, each of whom has, after his way, already used the
> machine as a scoring to his composing, as a script to its vocalization.
> It is now only a matter of the recognition of the conventions of com-
> position by field for us to bring into being an open verse as formal as
> the closed, with all its traditional advantages.
>
> If a contemporary poet leaves a space as long as the phrase before it,
> he means that space to be held, by the breath, an equal length of time.
> If he suspends a word or syllable at the end of a line (this was mostly
> cummings' addition) he meant that time to pass that it takes the eye—
> that hair of time suspended—to pick up the next line. If he wishes a
> pause so light it hardly separates the words, yet does not want a comma
> —which is an interruption of the meaning rather than the sounding
> of the line—follow him when he uses a symbol the typewriter has
> ready to hand:
> 'What does not change/ is the will to change'
> Observe him, when he takes advantage of the machine's multiple
> margins, to juxtapose:

[1] Robert Creeley (ed.), *Charles Olson, Selected Writings*, 1950, p. 18.

'Sd he:
   to dream takes no effort
    to think is easy
     to act is more difficult
      but for a man to act after he has taken thought, this !
is the most difficult thing of all'

Each of these lines is a progressing of both the meaning and the breathing forward, and then a backing up, without a progress or any kind of movement outside the unit of time local to the idea.

There is more to be said in order that this convention be recognized, especially in order that the revolution out of which it came may be so forwarded that work will get published to offset the reaction now afoot to return verse to inherited forms of cadence and rime. But what I want to emphasize here, by this emphasis on the typewriter as the personal and instantaneous recorder of the poet's work, is the already projective nature of verse as the sons of Pound and Williams are practising it. Already they are composing as though verse was to have the reading its writing involved, as though not the eye but the ear was to be its measurer, as though the intervals of its composition could be so carefully put down as to be precisely the intervals of its registration. For the ear, which once had the burden of memory to quicken it (rime and regular cadence were its aids and have merely lived on in print after the oral necessities were ended) can now again, that the poet has his means, be the threshold of projective verse.[1]

Robert Creeley has used the device of Composition by Field to great effect in short, lucid, meditative poems, such as

Here

What
has happened
makes

the world.
Live
on the edge,

looking.[2]

Here the poetry is all in the pauses, in the quality of attention that these pauses direct towards the words and syllables, in the control of speed. Creeley (like Olson, William Carlos Williams, and cummings) has discovered that a statement may be presented either as poetry or as prose, and that the poetic version can be made so by simply arranging for the

[1] ibid., pp. 22–24.   [2] Robert Creeley, *Words*. Scribners 1967, p. 128.

reader/listener to dwell upon the syllables and the silences. A great deal of contemporary poetry uses the techniques developed by this group of poets, and especially by Olson whose connection with Black Mountain College has led some critics to talk of a 'Black Mountain School' of poetry, though, in fact, many of the mannerisms and devices of the Black Mountain poets first appeared many years earlier in Ezra Pound, William Carlos Williams, and e. e. cummings.

What at first looks like a logical development from the notion that 'the poetry is in the pauses' is the Found Poem, though, again, this really arrived early in the century and was another product of the Surrealist movement. The Found Poem is simply an exact quotation from a piece of prose that has been so organized on the page as to appear to be a poem. Here is an example found by Shirley Kaufman in Sir John Lubbock's book *The Beauties of Nature*.

Rising and Sinking
(from the Beauties of Nature, by Sir John Lubbock, F.R.S.)

> The Welsh Mountains are older than the Vosges,
> The Vosges than the Pyrenees,
> The Pyrenees than the Alps,
> And the Alps than the Andes.
> Scandinavia is rising in the north,
> And sinking at the south.
> South America is rising on the west
> And sinking in the east.
> Slow subterranean movements
> Are still in progress.

SHIRLEY KAUFMAN[1]

From the Found Poem to the Collage Poem is only a step. The Collage Poem is one made by putting together found fragments, sometimes from one author or book, sometimes from several. Here is a Collage Poem from the Letters of George Bernard Shaw, by R. A. Sabell

Collage frcm G.B.S.

> Are the things I say true or not
> What does it matter whether I believe them or not
> I am alone, and yet there is a detestable, cool devil
> Seated in my chair telling me that all this is sincere lying
> I keep my word in spite of your whisper
> But I am not satisfied, there is a crumple in the rose.[2]

[1] In George Hitchcock (ed.), *Losers Weepers*. Kayak 1969, p. 15.
[2] In *Poetry 405* (1967), a gathering of student work from the members of Creative Writing classes at the University of Victoria. Privately Printed.

Yet another innovation of our century is Concrete Poetry, in which it is the visual, rather than auditory organization of the words, syllables, and letters which provides the poetic impact. Many Concrete Poems are, unfortunately, little more than pictures made up of letters and carry almost no 'message'. Some, however, utilize quite brilliantly the devices of space and verbal repetition. Here is a concrete poem by Paul de Vree

```
        a  rose  is  everywhere
        a  rose
as      a  rose
                for  ever  is
        a  rose
                for  ever  everywhere
        a  rose¹
```

This poem makes a connected statement. Alan Riddell's concrete poem[2] simply provides a play upon one word, 'revolver', and directs our attention to 'evolve' as one of its constituents.

Other concrete poems follow the line taken by Max Bense, who wrote.

This is a kind of poetry which produces neither the semantic nor the aesthetic sense of its elements, words for example, through the traditional formation of linear and grammatically ordered contexts, but which insists upon visual and surface connectives. So it is not the awareness of words following one after the other that is its primary constructive principle, but perception of their togetherness. The word is not used primarily as an intentional carrier of meaning. Beyond that it is used as a material element of construction in such a way that meaning and structure reciprocally express and determine each other. Simultaneity of the semantic and aesthetic functions of words occurs on the basis of simultaneous exploitation of all the material dimensions of the linguistic elements which, of course, can also appear to be broken up into syllables, sounds, morphemes or letters to express the aesthetic dependence of the language upon their analytical and syntactical possibilities. In this sense it is the constructive principle of concrete poetry alone which uncovers the material wealth of language.

Whatever consists of signs can be transmitted; that is, it is the subject, emission, perception and apperception of a communication scheme that can typify a specific design pattern which concrete poetry

[1] Mary Ellen Solt (ed.), *Concrete Poetry: A World View*. Indiana University Press 1968, p. 179.
[2] Alan Riddell, *Revolver*, in *The Malahat Review*, No. 27. 1973. University of Victoria, British Columbia.

revolver revolver revolver revolver revolver revolver revolver revolver can show. Let us now enlarge the concept of concrete poetry. Concrete texts are often closely related to poster texts due to their reliance upon typography and visual effect; that is, their aesthetic communications scheme often corresponds to that of advertisements. The central sign, often a word, takes on polemical or proclaiming function.

Concrete poetry does not entertain. It holds the possibility of fascination, and fascination is a form of concentration, that is of concentration which includes perception of the material as well as apperception of its meaning.[1]

Bense clearly would agree with Augusto de Camps that makers of Concrete Poetry begin by 'Assuming that the historical cycle of verse (as formal-rhythmical unit) is closed'. Thus the most 'pure' concrete poetry has little to do with 'poetry' as we normally think of it. Pierre and Ilse Garnier created 'Text for a Building'[2] in such a way that it is pure design using only one word, 'cinema'.

cinemacinemacinemacinemacinemacinemacinem
acinemacinemacinemacinemacinemacinemacin

and so on.

This movement may seem to many poets to have gone so far towards pure visual design and so far away from the presentation of meaning as to have ceased to be concerned with poetry at all. Nevertheless the Concrete Poetry Movement is another matter with which the poet of our time has to come to terms. It may be that, while he does not wish to become a full-blooded writer of Concrete Poetry, he may find some of the devices useful. After all, we can find examples of near-concrete poetry in George Herbert (*Easter Wings*) and in Dylan Thomas (*Vision and Prayer*) and in many poems from the seventeenth to the nineteenth century in which memorial verses are ingeniously arranged so as to present the image of a cross, or an urn.

From the visual extreme of concrete poetry it is perhaps reasonable to turn to poetry which is almost entirely auditory. There are some poems which are concerned less with meaning than with the organization of patterns of sound. Edith Sitwell was one of the first twentieth-century poets to attempt this kind of 'pure' poetry in her suite, *Façade*, in which the sound is more important than the sense. Consider her poem *The Wind's Bastinado*[3]

[1] Mary Ellen Solt, op. cit., p. 73.
[2] ibid., p. 163.
[3] Edith Sitwell, *Collected Poems*. Macmillan 1957, p. 127.

The wind's bastinado
Whipt on the calico
Skin of the Macaroon
And the black Picaroon
Beneath the galloon
Of the midnight sky.
Came the great Soldan
In his sedan
Floating his fan—
Saw what the sly
Shadow's cocoon
In the barracoon
Held. Out they fly.
'This melon,
Sir Mammon,
Comes out of Babylon:
Buy for a patacoon—
Sir, you must buy!'
Said Il Magnifico
Pulling a fico—
With a stoccado
And a gambado,
Making a wry
Face: 'This corraceous
Round orchidaceous
Laceous porraceous
Fruit is a lie!
It is my friend King Pharaoh's head
That nodding blew out of the Pyramid . . .'
The tree's small corinths
Were hard as jacinths,
For it is winter and cold winds sigh . . .
No nightingale
In her farthingale
Of bunched leaves let her singing die.

The element of 'meaning' here is not very important. The poem is a
fantasy, and a piece of verbal music, mouth-music. Another poet who
uses sound in an even more extreme fashion is Michael McClure. He
prefaced his *Ghost Tantras* with the statement:

You've never heard anything like this before. These are my personal
songs but anyone can sing them. Pronounce them as they are spelled
and don't worry about details—use a natural voice and let the vibrations

occur. They come from a swirling ball of silence that melds with outer sounds and thought. They were written in kitchens and bedrooms and frontrooms and airplanes and a couple in Mexico City. Their purpose is to bring beauty and change the shape of the universe.[1]

GOOOOOOR ! GOOOOOOOOOO !
GOOOOOOOOOOR !
GRAHHH ! GRAHH ! GRAHH !
Grah gooooooor ! Ghahh ! Graaarr ! Greeeeer ! Grayowhr !
Greeeeee
GRAHHRR ! RAHHR ! GRAHHHR ! GAHHR ! HRAHR !
BE NOT SUGAR BUT BE LOVE
looking for sugar
GAHHHHHHHHHHHHHHHHHHHHHHHHHHHH !
ROWRR !
GROOOOOOOOOOOOOOOOOOOOOOOOOOOOOOOOOH ![2]

It is not easy to sum up the situation in poetry today for, as I have said, there are many 'schools' and 'styles' and labels are always approximate. I would however suggest that MacNeice's poem could be said to belong to a 'Classical' tradition in that it utilizes all the conventional methods of metre, rhyme, and alliteration in a connected manner and in orthodox syntax. Ted Hughes' poem belongs to that kind of poetry which is dependent for its effect upon pseudo-ritual and incantation, and the reworking of or renewing of structures and formulae that can be found in much primitive oral literature and even in the rhyming games and skipping and ball-bouncing songs of children. I would therefore suggest that this kind of poetry might be called *Tribal*, for it derives from the oral poetry of the tribe and the word *tribal* suggests its origins in earlier forms of society. Roethke, Lowell, Sexton and others have been labelled 'Confessional' though I would prefer the term *Egoist*, to suggest the distinction that these first-person monologues are deeply interested in the proposition of philosophical Egoism that, to use Webster's formulation, 'the individual consciousness alone is knowable', and to remove the suggestion that the poems are necessarily factually autobiographical. The work of cummings (and, indeed of Williams, and Pound) seems to me to be loosely such that it can reasonably be given Olson's label of *Open Field Poetry*. McClure's 'mouth music' belongs, I think, to a school we might call *Ideophonic* as

[1] Michael McClure, *Ghost Tantras*. City Lights 1967, p. (iii).
[2] ibid., p. 7.

it is not concerned with the written but with the spoken word, while Concrete Poetry is clearly in what some of its practitioners have already labelled as an *Ideogrammatic* tradition.

The labels are, of course, only of use in enabling us to sort out the main movements and approaches of poetry. They cannot safely be attached to individual poets, for poets often change their approaches from poem to poem. cummings has, after all, written 'Classical' poetry and MacNeice has written 'Tribal' poetry, and many poets have written occasional ideogrammatic poetry who could not reasonably be called ideogrammatic poets.

I have attempted to identify only a small number of poetic approaches —Classical, Tribal, Egoist, Open Field, Ideophonic, and Ideogrammatic. I could easily have gone on to suggest others, to discuss poems based not upon stress-count but syllable-count, to discuss the Imagist and Objectivist tradition in which the poems are made by the juxtaposition of images and all 'editorial' comment and 'argument' is excluded, as in some of the work of William Carlos Williams, Louis Zukowsky, and George Oppen. I could have considered the approach to poetry made by the Futurists, and presented examples of 'Pop' poetry. My purpose, however, has been less to provide encyclopaedic coverage than to indicate what I consider the main trends, and to show how the poet, in reading the work of others, is concerned to learn new ways of exploration and expression. I have also been intent upon showing how the poet today is faced with an embarrassment of riches in his search for new techniques.

The poem, however, is not, to the poet or to anybody else, simply a collection of technical devices. The techniques are useless if they are not an integral part of the whole poem, if the content and form are not so closely inter-related as to form a unity. Let me finish this chapter, therefore, by presenting one final poem in the Classical tradition, and showing how form and content relate to each other. The poem is George Barker's *Allegory of the Adolescent and the Adult*[1]

> It was when weather was Arabian I went
> Over the downs to Alton where winds were wounded
> With flowers and swathed me with aroma, I walked
> Like Saint Christopher Columbus through a sea's welter
> Of gaudy ways looking for a wonder.

[1] George Barker, *Collected Poems 1930–1955*. Faber 1957, pp. 62–63.

Who was I, who knows, no one when I started,
No more than the youth who takes longish strides,
Gay with a girl and obstreperous with strangers,
Fond of some songs, not unusually stupid,
I ascend hills anticipating the strange.

Looking for a wonder I went on a Monday,
Meandering over the Alton down and moor;
When was it I went, an hour a year or more,
That Monday back, I cannot remember.
I only remember I went in a gay mood.

Hollyhock here and rock and rose there were,
I wound among them knowing they were no wonder;
And the bird with a worm and the fox in a wood
Went flying and flurrying in front, but I was
Wanting a worse wonder, a rarer one.

So I went on expecting miraculous catastrophe.
What is it, I whispered, shall I capture a creature
A woman for a wife, or find myself a king,
Sleep and awake to find Sleep is my kingdom?
How shall I know my marvel when it comes?

Then after long striding and striving I was where
I had so long longed to be, in the world's wind,
At the hill's top, with no more ground to wander
Excepting downward, and I had found no wonder.
Found only the sorrow that I had missed my marvel.

Then I remembered, was it the bird or worm,
The hollyhock, the flower or the strong rock,
Was it the mere dream of the man and woman
Made me a marvel? It was not. It was
When on the hilltop I stood in the world's wind.

The world is my wonder, where the wind
Wanders like wind, and where the rock is
Rock. And man and woman flesh on a dream.
I look from my hill with the woods behind,
And Time, a sea's chaos, below.

If we mean by 'allegory' a narrative in which each character and object
can be identified as representative of one definite quality, or given a

precise denotation, then this poem is no allegory. If we use the word loosely, meaning simply a fable or parable, then the title is meaningful and has been given an appropriate quality of incantatory exuberance by the use of the three chiming As.

The fable itself is straightforward enough. We all go through our adolescence looking for marvels; true maturity begins when we realize that the whole process of our living, and of our questioning it, is a wonder—and all the earth miraculous.

This poem has enhanced its theme with freshness and immediacy in several ways. Local and particular references ('to Alton', 'on a Monday') though unimportant thematically, are valuable as gestures that stage the poem's events in our own world of the actual and commonplace. The references to Christopher Columbus and to Arabia operate similarly, the first presenting an aura of the heroic and introducing a suggestion of the far-ranging nature of the journey that is to take place; and the second promoting those notions of the marvellous that are so often connected with Arabia, as Walter de la Mare was clever enough to perceive when he composed his irrational but haunting lyric. These elements of the heroic and the marvellous are also present in the third stanza where the supernormal time-dimension of magical experience is implied, and there are deliberate, though not over serious, references to the romance themes of maiden, king, and fairy kingdom in stanza five. These comparatively unobtrusive allusions do their work well, but the main work of the poem is done by its astonishing alliterative and assonant patterns.

In the first five stanzas all the end words are linked with each other by alliteration, first in w, and then in st, m, w, and hard c or k. These stanzas combine to form one uninterrupted surge of narrative excitement; there is no check to the journey or to the hope for a miracle until the last line of the sixth stanza, where the end word breaks the alliterative pattern, and doubt intrudes upon hope. The seventh stanza also checks the alliterative flow of its second line with the word *rock*, which therefore obtrudes, hard and rocklike, at a point where doubt is intensified. The eighth and final stanza discards the previous alliterative pattern completely and presents a new one, just as the speaker himself substitutes for his earlier unthinking, adolescent hope a more mature and sturdily intellectual acceptance of life's realities. Thus the sound pattern of the poem, as revealed merely in the end words, reflects and intensifies the thematic structure of the poem.

The sound is important in other respects also. The assonance and alliteration in the body of each stanza emphasize the incantatory element in the speaker's reflections and thus intensify our appreciation of the self-intoxicating aspect of the theme. Moreover, by making all the ideas and images appear subordinate to the tune, it suggests that the whole of the speaker's world of perception is both dominated and obscured by his emotional excitement. And poems have to do with history, too, as well as with individual characterization; the alliterative techniques of this particular poem recall what might be called the adolescence of literature as well as the adolescence of the speaker, for they are reminiscent of Anglo-Saxon verse in which the lines were bound together by consonance and assonance rather than by metrical devices. This echoing of the largely heroic verse of the remote past is appropriate in a poem that continually trembles on the verge of epic exuberance.

The use of consonance and assonance is valuable for another reason: it allows the poem a wide freedom of rhythm while preserving the rhetorical advantages of disciplined form. Thus the (usually) four-beat lines include varying numbers of unstressed syllables; and their rhythms, too, vary, as do those of Gerard Manley Hopkins, between the iambic (or trochaic) and the anapaestic (or dactylic) with occasional emphatic spondees. This results in an apparent spontaneity, even recklessness—which is, again, appropriate to the theme and expressive of it.

The poem as a whole makes use of the notion of a wanderer in a particular landscape who, at his journey's end, which is also the end of his meditation, happens on a Truth. This is a Wordsworthian device, and we may well be reminded of at least the opening movements of both *Michael* and *Resolution and Independence*. The conclusion, however, is not Wordsworthian, but more Bergsonian. We are marvellous because we are part of the impulse of all creation toward immortality, and because man is the highest manifestation of the yearning of the spirit of life. As time rose once out of chaos, so we now rise out of time, making it seem a chaos from which we have escaped and climbed as life itself, aeons ago, climbed out of the sea.

In saying this I am not only summing up the poem's final statement but also summarizing its total structure. The fluid and incantatory qualities of its beginning reflect more than the emotionalism of adolescence; they reflect also the flux of life itself in its origins. Moreover, the way in which intuitive excitement is checked by intellectual stirrings, which lead to a harder and more definite attitude, must be regarded as a statement about the evolution of mankind as well as the maturing of an individual. In addition, just as the speaker of the poem must finally recognize the marvel of his own existence, so mankind must realize its possession of divinity, and the poet itself understand the miraculous nature of his own artistry and of the conquest of art over time.

George Barker has written many fine poems—but this is perhaps his most extraordinary lyric achievement, and one of the master poems of our time in its total fusion of message and structure.[1]

---

[1] This examination of *Allegory of the Adolescent and the Adult* first appeared in Oscar Williams (ed.), *Master Poems of the English Language*, Trident Press 1966, pp. 1037–1041.

EIGHT The Problem of Poetic Authority[1]

I referred earlier to the truly dedicated poet who spends his life labouring towards the creation of a major work, a large-scale poem or epic. It is difficult for a poet to convince himself (or indeed anyone else) that he has the necessary authority to speak out on matters of importance. He may attempt to speak with an air of authority, but he has little real status in the social system. If his authority is questioned he may point to his other work, and suggest that, as a professor, or publisher, or businessman, or farmer, he is a person whose opinions should carry some weight. He cannot, however, derive the justification for his authoritative manner entirely from his poethood, unless his questioners are all members of the poetic fraternity.

In other times poets were able to speak with an authority born of their acknowledged position and function in society, as well as with the authority of those accepted as being divinely 'possessed' or 'inspired'. In other times and other cultures the poet was priest, historian, genealogist, philosopher, and medicine-man. He both affected and recorded the history of his society. In the Middle Ages in Europe the poet's functions were never in doubt, and his social position, which was psychologically if not financially secure, also gave him a certain freedom. Moreover, his various functions were so well understood that he could easily indicate which one he was, at a given time, engaged in performing by adopting a particular diction or verse form. It was accepted that certain forms and modes of speech were proper for serious and state affairs, that others were appropriate to verse and to entertain a popular audience, and that, in certain modes and *genres* a number of conventional phrases, locutions, and devices were inevitable. This enabled the poet to indicate the area or *genre* in which his poem was operating, with great economy of

[1] This chapter first appeared, in a slightly different form, as *W. B. Yeats: The Poet as Synopsis,* in *Mosaic,* Volume I, Number I, The University of Manitoba Press, October 1967.

means; it also enabled him to mix different dictions to more effect than is possible when there is no clear demarcation line between one diction and another. This state of affairs clearly existed in England up to the end of the sixteenth century.

When we look from the poets of the Middle Ages, and from Dunbar and Skelton, to the poetry of later periods, the problem of authority becomes clearer. One might even say that the poets of each decade had a slightly different answer to the question 'What authority have you?' In the eighteenth century some pointed to sheer craftsmanship in verse, and some to sociological justifications. In the Romantic period some elaborated notions of the poet as a pseudo-prophet, and some of the poet as *Homo Patiens*.

In the late nineteenth and early twentieth centuries the problem became acute. The followers of the Romantics had worn out the notion of the poet as the embodiment of a transcendentally pure and suffering soul. Justification by subject-matter was again replacing justification by sensibility. Henley and Davidson, in their different ways, began to present the poet as a critic of society. Browning's poet in his 'scrutinizing hat', with his powerful psychological insights, began to be in vogue. The 'Art for Art's Sake' movement—the aestheticism of the eighties, and the so-called *fin-de-siècle* decadence and sensationalism of the nineties —can be regarded as either a reactionary trend, or the last fling of the believers in 'Authority from Sensibility'. By the end of the first decade of the twentieth century, the movement towards finding authority for the poet by subject-matter had really taken over; moreover the subject-matter had to be sociological in tendency.

One cannot, of course, present a general solution to this problem. Every poet will attempt to solve it in his own way and in terms of his own particular interests. Pound built his authority essentially upon the notion of 'authority by subject matter', making his Cantos encyclopaedic in range and filling them with discussions of history, economics, and the rise and fall of civilizations. Nikos Katzanzakis created his great poem by basing it upon Homer and extending the Homeric epic. William Carlos Williams attempted to construct a universal myth of human society around a typical American city, which he called *Paterson*. In order to see this whole matter of Poetic Authority clearly it is perhaps wise to take the case of one poet and see how he solved, or failed to solve, the problem of acquiring the Authority to speak out, acquiring the position of Master-Poet.

W. B. Yeats began his writing career in the last years of the nineteenth century and in the shadow of late romanticism. A lonely, dreamy, rather frail child, whose brilliant artist father took a strongly Pre-Raphaelite view of literature, his natural tendency was to consider that the poet's sensibility need be his only justification. The splendour of his dreams justified his social arrogance

> . . . When I was young,
> I had not given a penny for a song
> Did not the poet sing it with such airs
> That one believed he had a sword upstairs . . .
>
> (*All Things Can Tempt Me*)

Nevertheless, there was continually in his heart a hankering after a more solid justification. Perhaps on account of the Morris influence, perhaps because of his Irishness, he spent much time finding and founding small societies in which he could operate as a significant figure. Small societies of adepts tempted him greatly, as one can easily see from his attitude towards the Rhymers, the Society of the Golden Dawn, and his stories in *The Secret Rose*. Yeats also involved himself in the Nationalist movement, and did yeoman service by editing and presenting folk-stories and folk-tales, thus establishing the fact that the Irish race had, indeed, a 'Sword upstairs'. When Lady Gregory's *Cuchullain of Muirthemne* appeared in 1904 he called it 'the finest book that has come out of Ireland in my time'. This was because it gave the community poet the store of material that traditionally was his; he could now celebrate the glories of the tribe, those glories having been rediscovered, and thus emulate the socially secure poet of earlier periods.

Tradition and the idea of tradition meant a great deal to Yeats. Indeed, a part of his answer to the Authority problem was to indicate the poet's position in a number of traditions, and his possession of a multiple-stranded heritage. One tradition was, of course, the Neo-Platonic so exhaustively discussed by F. A. C. Wilson; it was not, however, the only one. The Dun Emer and Cuala Presses, of which Yeats acted as Editor from their inception to his death, also reflected his sense of heritage; these, directly bequeathed him by William Morris, were part of that notion of the select audience and the court poet, the fine manuscript and the devoted scribe, which was important to his highly idealistic picture of the Middle Ages. Numerous other ways in which Yeats provided himself, and his role, with an ancestry can easily be listed: his genealogical concern with the Butlers, Pollexfens, Middletons; his pseudo-scholarly devotion to the idea of a great 'line' of Irish Scholars and

Orators—Swift, Burke, Grattan, Goldsmith; his own continual pretension to scholarship, and his love of an old book; his delight in the
Samurai sword given him by Sato, and his passionate concern for the
old Tower he could rebuild, are some of them. His discovery that one of
his poems had become a popular 'folk song', whose author's name had
been forgotten, made him feel that he had become so much a part of the
country that only his work remained; he had become one with the
authors of *Chevy Chase*, and *Ichom of Irlonde*, a poem which he used himself, extending it, becoming part of it, in order to feel himself one with
the great voice of past singers.

Nevertheless, however assiduously Yeats contrived these bracing
bulwarks of tradition for his none-too-ivory tower, the problem of
Authority is not answered for a poet by his beliefs about his role, but by
his performance of it, and it is here that Yeats reveals his greatness.
No poet had adopted the stance Yeats felt proper for a great number of
years. He was obliged to rewrite the whole script around a new character, the twentieth-century Master-Poet.

It is here that the problem of diction again presents itself. What was
the correct language for a Master-Poet? Diction should, perhaps, indicate the social levels on which the poem is working, but in the late
nineteenth and early twentieth centuries the language of most poetry
seemed entirely divorced from the language used for other purposes.
Moreover, there was no clear pattern of conventional usage to enable a
poet to imply, by means of his vocabulary or tone, the nature of his
poetic stance. This problem, the consequence of the break-up of the
medieval pattern, and, later, of the Romantic revolution against the
eighteenth-century Neo-Classical conventions which had, in part, re-
placed it, had become even more severe with the years. It had become so
severe, indeed, that Browning had been obliged to invent an individual
diction of his own, which he could lard with social pointers. Hardy had
also created an inimitable manner, as had Davidson. These poets, however, had the actual personality of the *Makar* less in the forefront of their
subject-matter than Yeats. Yeats, who had seen the Artist as Hero (and the
Hero as some kind of Artist) from his earliest days, had the Poet as one
of his central themes. In Yeats' lyrical work from its beginnings to 1910
one can see a tension between his growing concept of the Master-Poet
persona, and his inherited Post-Romantic and Pre-Raphaelitic diction.
The earliest poems have typically Post-Romantic phrases, words, and
locutions. Yeats' revision of them was often an attempt to harden the
diction and thus alter the *persona*.

Nevertheless, even in the first versions of the poems published before 1910, one can see the hard, bare, colloquial diction rubbing shoulders with the decadent Romantic style and cadence. Specific Irishisms ('When I was a boy with never a crack in my heart') exist alongside pastoral affectations ('The woods of Arcady are dead', 'the hapless faun') in *The Wanderings of Oisin* (1889). Attempts at folk-ballads jostle attempts at eclogue. In *The Countess Kathleen* (1892) some attempt is made to create a single *persona* who could be both court and folk poet. In *Apologia addressed to Ireland in the coming days* there are references to the speaker as part of a tradition which is at once nationalist and druidic

> Know that I would accounted be
> True brother of that company
> Who sang to sweeten Ireland's wrong,
> Ballad and story, rann and song;
> Nor be I any less of them
> Because the red rose bordered hem
> Of her whose history began ˙
> Before God made the angelic clan,
> Trails all about the written page, . . .
>
> Nor may I less be counted one
> With David, Mangan, Ferguson,
> Because to him who ponders well,
> My rhymes more than their rhymings tell . . .

There is also a reference to Ireland as a 'Druid Land'. Now all this can be seen as the product of a bad conscience; Yeats felt he should be writing political and folk poetry, but found himself writing mystical poetry. This may be partly true, but I think it would be more true to say that Yeats, venturing for the first time upon any kind of extended 'public' statement of his own function as a poet, was really more interested in making the speaker of the poem a successful fiction than in defending his own attitudes. Certainly, in the next volume, *The Wind Among the Reeds*, we get the *persona* of the speaker presented carefully in the third person. Thus we have poems in which a Lover-Poet speaks: *Aedh tells of the Rose in His Heart*, *Aedh to Dectora*, *Michael Robartes remembers*, and so forth. These titles were revised later to read: *The Lover tells of the Rose in his heart*, *The Lover mourns for the Loss of Love*, and *He remembers Forgotten Beauty*; these later titles deliberately recall the stance of the medieval courtly poet, and remind us of the titling used by Synge in his translations from Petrarch. The first titles were supported by notes on the personalities mentioned, and by a whole scenario of story and allusion. The last named poem, indeed, started off its life as *O'Sullivan Rua to Mary Lavell*, but Robartes proved a more satisfactory notion.

Thus Yeats has done what he so often did—created a drama in which certain songs could be made, certain debates conducted—in order to provide himself with a perspective conducive to poetry. Later the scenario can be shelved and the songs remembered. This is, of course, largely what he did with *A Vision*; it was an enabling device. Such devices allowed Yeats to hide his own personal involvement in the attitudes he was presenting, or to leave unanswered, even by himself, the question of the extent to which he agreed with the statements made. This is often wise for a poet; if all his statements are made in the first person he may begin to worry over whether he believes in the opinions his poems express and forget to worry over whether or not he fully assents to their structures. Yeats certainly worked frequently in this way, and one often finds a character anticipating views and attitudes of a speaker who is later presented as if he were the poet himself.

I say 'as if he were' because it is my contention that 'Yeats' is as much of an invention as the fictional speakers he labelled as Michael Robartes and Crazy Jane. I would even say that the creation of a significant and highly individual 'Poet-as-Speaker' is Yeats' most important single dramatic and poetic achievement. Others have, of course, manufactured similar *personae*: Donne is an obvious example as also is the Byron of *Don Juan*. Yeats' invention, however, is more complex than theirs and it developed additional complexities over the years.

One can easily see this development taking place. In revising *The Wind Among the Reeds*, Yeats not only removed the references to Aedh and O'Sullivan Rua and Michael Robartes, but rearranged the poems of which they had, originally, been the speakers into two groups, one spoken by The Lover, and one by The Poet. This later recasting makes a second look at the poems spoken by The Poet advisable. They are slight, and include references to 'passionate rhyme', to the working at 'poor rhymes' 'day out, day in', and to the poets (it is implied) as both courageous and proud. They are called a 'lonely, proud, winged multitude' in *To his Heart, bidding it have no Fear* which was first published under another title in 1896. From 1899 to 1921 it was called *To My heart bidding it have no Fear*. It was altered to the present title in the collection of Later Poems in 1922.

In the next collection of Lyrics, *In the Seven Woods* (1903), the *persona* has begun to emerge more clearly. Though the poems are described as

'chiefly of the Irish Heroic Age' only two of the thirteen poems involved a fictive speaker in their first printings—Red Hanrahan and
Echtge—and in the book itself only Red Hanrahan remained. In this
book, too, there is the poem *Adam's Curse*, which, though in dialogue
form, is Yeats' second attempt at explicit lyrical statement upon his
role as poet. The first version of 1902 contains the lines:

> I said 'a line will take us hours maybe,
> Yet if it does not seem a moment's thought
> Our stitching and unstitching has been naught.
> Better go down upon your marrow bones
> And scrub a kitchen pavement or break stones
> Like an old pauper in all kinds of weather;
> For to articulate sweet sounds together
> Is to work harder than all these and yet
> Be thought an idler by the noisy set
> Of bankers, schoolmasters, and clergymen
> The martyrs call the world.'

This poem, emphasizing that

> . . . It's certain there is no fine thing
> Since Adam's fall but needs much labouring. . . .

also emphasizes the poet's opposition to the machinery of Commerce,
Education, and Religion, and allies him with the 'martyrs'. It is clear,
too, that the poet's craft is supposed to result in 'sweet sounds' that
must appear occasional, spontaneous, impromptu.

This is, of course, a lyric stance. In the same collection, however, we
get the ceremonial *The Players Ask for a Blessing on the Psalteries and Themselves* which ends

> The proud and careless notes live on
> But bless our hands that ebb away.

It appears as if the poet must somehow combine deliberate labour, and
even ceremonious speech-making, with impromptu lyric utterance. The
diction of *Adam's Curse* is tougher than that of many previous poems,
however. The speaker has observed scullery-maids as well as mystical
Roses, and is capable of an almost vulgar directness of speech.

The next important collection of short poems that Yeats produced is
The Green Helmet of 1910. Between 1903 and 1910 he had published
several plays, and had rearranged, selected, collected, revised, and re-
shaped his earlier poems in several ways. *The Green Helmet* is a most

important collection, for in it Yeats moves forward towards the vigour of language which is typical of his later work, and which is central to the understanding of his fully achieved *persona*.

I have argued elsewhere that much of this shift in tone, and this new directness and harshness may be due to Yeats having read the unpublished poems of Synge in 1908. Whether or not this is true, there is certainly a great change here. The book in its first, Cuala Press, edition is divided into three sections. The first is headed 'Raymond Lully and his Wife Pernella' and contains poems which stem directly from Yeats's love for Maud Gonne. They are some of his most obviously personal poems, and it is interesting that Yeats thought it necessary to disguise them thus. He may (though it does not seem likely) have wished to avoid embarrassing Maud Gonne. But I feel that, though this may be part of it, the fundamental cause was his intense need to have even his most personal poems spoken by a created person distinct from himself. Poetry must be spoken through a mask, by an invented *persona*.

The second section of the book was originally called *Momentary Thoughts*, and in this section Yeats takes up his notion of creating apparently impromptu lyrics. The section opens with yet another poem about the poet's role and craft

> The fascination of what's difficult
> Has dried the sap out of my veins, and rent
> Spontaneous joy and natural content
> Out of my heart . . .

This, however, is followed, after two epigrams, by the un-Petrarchan poem with the Petrarchan title, *To a Poet who would have me Praise certain Bad Poets, Imitators of His and Mine*. And after another five poems, in the penultimate poem of the section, we read:

> All things can tempt me from this craft of verse:
> One time it was a woman's face, or worse——
> The seeming needs of my fool-driven land . . .

This contrasts sharply with both the tone and the sentiment of the first section. The voice is harsh, and the note direct. The poet is not a martyr now, but a fighter, a man on the move. Now the poet is justifying himself by his opposition, by his individual strength, but also by his new understanding of the multiple nature of his tradition.

The poems published in 1914 and thereafter can usefully be regarded as forming a kind of unity. I do not mean that they all make use of the same *persona*, or that they all deal with similar subjects, but that their variety, and their apparent inconsistency, can be regarded as forming part of one overmastering intention. This intention can be summarized in the words of Synge, often quoted by Yeats, who said that the poet should make 'the whole of life' his subject-matter. It can also be summarized as a deliberate attempt at syncretism: the discovery of antinomies and oppositions and the combining of them into one whole which could be represented by a single *persona*. This *persona* reveals itself in terms both of the poet's canon, and of the speaker of a small number of key poems which openly attempt syncretism in either personal or objective terms.

The first poem, *The Grey Rock*, of *Responsibilities* (1914) is itself an attempt to identify the multiple tradition in which the poet should work and includes these significant lines addressed to the members of The Rymers Club

> You kept the Muses' sterner laws,
> And unrepenting faced your ends,
> And therefore earned the right—and yet
> Dowson and Johnson most I praise—
> To troop with those the world's forgot,
> And copy their proud steady gaze.

The book itself places poems about the heroic past alongside poems of the present, but the latter are always related to the past. Thus we get in one poem the challenging colloquialism of

> You gave but will not give again
> Until enough of Paudeen's pence
> By Biddy's halfpennies have lain
> To be 'some sort of evidence',
> Before you'll put your guineas down . . .

though the word *lain* has a slightly formal and archaic air, and *guineas* and *pence* are not part of a completely vulgar diction, the passage is dominated by the wish to speak in forceful everyday tones. Later on, however, we get

> What cared Duke Ercole, that bid
> His mummers to the market-place,
> What th'onion-sellers thought or did
> So that his Plautus set the pace
> For the Italian comedies ?
> And Guidabaldo, when he made
> That grammar school of courtesies

Where wit and beauty learned their trade
Upon Urbino's windy hill,
Had sent no runners to and fro
That he might learn the shepherds' will.

Here the references and the diction are far from vulgar in their overall
effect. Nevertheless, there are colloquial elements, such as the commonplace *learned their trade*, and *set the pace* and the deliberately anachronistic
grammar school. In the diction of this poem, as in that of the majority of
Yeats' later poems, the formal and archaic is set beside the colloquial
and contemporary; vulgarisms are juxtaposed with pedanticisms; slang
and ceremony co-exist. Yeats was fully aware of this aspect of his diction,
and commented upon it, both directly and obliquely, several times. It is
one aspect of his syncretic method, and one way in which he attempted
to fuse the 'dream of the noble' with that of the 'beggar man', the poet
as scholar fusing with the poet as street-singer or vulgar minstrel.

In *The Wild Swans at Coole* (1919) Yeats developed his syncretic
approach further. *In Memory of Robert Gregory* not only presents the speaker
as partaking of the insights of both scholar and common man by mixing
its diction, but attempts to group together disparate and conflicting
attitudes by celebrating the memory of friends who embodied them.
Robert Gregory himself is portrayed as 'Our Sidney and our perfect
man'. He was a countryman and a lover of the countryside. He was a
painter, who

> . . . understood
> All work in metal or in wood,
> In moulded plaster or in carven stone . . .
> Soldier, scholar, horseman, he,
> And all he did done perfectly
> As though he had but that one trade alone.

By being this twentieth-century version of the complete Renaissance
gentleman, Robert Gregory was 'all life's epitome'. Thus we can see
that 'the whole of life' to Yeats means the whole of life as presented
in one personality who fuses the present with the past, and combines all
the arts in one allmastering genius.

If we take Robert Gregory as a pattern of excellence, we can see most
of the parts of that pattern reflected in the other poems in *The Wild
Swans at Coole* which present love of the countryside, the attitude of the
soldier and horseman, and the viewpoint of the Classical scholar and of
the artist.

Alongside the use of unifying personalities in Yeats' work, however, we must recognize a similar use of divisive characters. Michael Robartes and Owen Aherne are two of these. Another two, in *Ego Dominus Tuus*, are simply labelled Hic and Ille. A third pair are The Saint and The Hunchback in the poem of that name. This was, of course, the period during which Yeats was working on *A Vision* (1925) which he described, in its 1937 edition, as being 'stylistic arrangements of experience comparable to the cubes in the drawing of Wyndham Lewis and to the ovoids in the sculpture of Brancusi'. *A Vision* arranges history and presents both the movements of history and the nature of human personality in a number of categories, which relate to each other in a complex manner. The final intention, however, is not to present variety, but unity. There may be many 'phases of the moon' but, Yeats points out on page 193 of the 1956 edition of *A Vision*,

> The ultimate reality because neither one nor many concord nor discord, is symbolized by a phaseless sphere . . .

On page 213 he states

> I have now described many symbols which seem mechanical because united in a single structure, and of which the greater number, precisely because they tell always the same story, may seem unnecessary. Yet every symbol, except where it lies in vast periods of time and so beyond our experience, has evoked for me some form of human destiny, and that form, once evoked, has appeared everywhere, as if there were but one destiny, as my own form might appear in a room full of mirrors.

Again, on page 240, referring to the 'Phaseless sphere' or 'Thirteenth Cone', he says

> It becomes even conscious of itself as so seen, like some great dancer, the perfect flower of modern culture, dancing some primitive dance and conscious of his or her own life and the dance. . . . Only one symbol exists, though the reflecting mirrors make many appear and all different.

The one symbol that Yeats postulates is thus an image of syncretic unity. Apparent variety and apparent inconsistency are the result of different perspectives upon this one central reality.

Much of Yeats's work in *Michael Robartes and the Dancer* (1921), and *The Tower* (1928) is devoted to the discovery of this one symbol which will sum up, somehow or other, all phases of human experience, and therefore, also, all the different stances of poetry. Both the city of Byzantium and the Tower at Thoor Ballylee are investigated as candidates for the position. Byzantium, however, seems meaningful only in the context of a Neo-Platonic tradition. It is in the title poem of *The Tower* that the one symbol begins to emerge. Looking down from the battlements the speaker recalls the history of his country and the poets who have been involved in it and have celebrated it. Having done this and perceived the way in which the poet is both a vehicle of the Great Memory and a celebrant of passing beauty, a part of the passing scene, he moves on to consider his own position. He refers to the pride of his countrymen, to Burke and to Grattan, and then declares his faith.

> I mock Plotinus' thought
> And cry in Plato's teeth,
> Death and life were not
> Till man made up the whole,
> Made lock, stock and barrel
> Out of his bitter soul,
> Aye, sun and moon and star, all,
> And further add to that
> That, being dead, we rise,
> Dream and so create
> Translunar Paradise.
> I have prepared my peace
> With learned Italian things
> And the proud stones of Greece,
> Poet's imaginings
> And memories of love,
> Memories of the words of women,
> All those things whereof
> Man makes a superhuman
> Mirror-resembling dream.

Thus man is now seen as the true creator of his universe. Man as poet creates a dream which, like a mirror, or like many mirrors, reflects back different versions of the one face.

In *Meditations in Time of Civil War* which, significantly (for Yeats took pains over the arranging of his collections), is the next poem in *The Tower*, we are presented with the poet in the act of creating the mirrors. These reflect back to him ancient Greece, Ancestral Houses, Milton's *Il Penseroso*, Irish Soldiers of the Civil War, Japanese art and tradition, the countryside, unicorns, hawks, and Babylonian prophecies—to name but a few of the themes and images occurring to the speaker's mind. This activity of the poet, however, does not appear to solve the problem of his role in society, for the last stanza of the last section reads

> I turn away and shut the door, and on the stair
> Wonder how many times I could have proved my worth
> In something that all others understand or share;
> But O! Ambitious heart, had such a proof drawn forth
> A company of friends, a conscience set at ease,
> It had but made us pine the more. The abstract joy,
> The half-read wisdom of daemonic images
> Suffice the ageing man as once the growing boy.

In the following poem, *Nineteen Hundred and Nineteen*, we read

> Some moralist or mythological poet
> Compares the solitary soul to a swan;
> I am satisfied with that,
> Satisfied if a troubled mirror show it
> Before that brief gleam of its life be gone,
> An image of its state . . .

The state of the soul is compared not only to a swan in this poem, but also a dance for

> All men are dancers and their tread
> Goes to the barbarous clangour of a gong.

This may remind us of the description in *A Vision* of the 'phaseless sphere' as 'like some great dancer, the perfect flower of modern culture, dancing some primitive dance and conscious of his or her own life and the dance.' It also leads us past several poems dealing with specific reflections from the mirroring dream, to the poem *Among School Children* where the 'one symbol' is clearly identified in terms of both the flower and the dance, and in terms also of the central mirror-making *persona* of the poet himself. In this poem the autobiographical meditation, always central to Yeats' exploratory procedures, and a part of his inheritance from the Romantics, takes on new and important characteristics, becomes, in fact, a more than personal summary and synthesis of human experience.

The autobiographical structure of *Among School Children* has been commented upon often enough, and its philosophical content has also been well trampled. I am concerned to point out only one aspect of the poem. This is the nature, and range, of its references. In the first stanza we are in a twentieth-century Catholic School, where the children are being taught by nuns. In the second stanza we are referred to the myth of Leda and the Swan, a myth which explains the downfall of one civilization and the foundation of another. We are also referred to Plato, a philosopher who is one of the founders of our way of thinking. The third stanza fuses the image of Helen of Troy with that of Maud Gonne and a child in the schoolroom. The fourth stanza moves us briefly into another period and another civilization with its reference to the *Quattrocento*. The fifth and sixth stanzas move between the speaker's present and the past of Porphyry, Aristotle, Plato and Pythagoras. In the seventh stanza the Greek and the Christian myths are brought together with additional references to timeless maternal emotions. The poem concludes with the stanza which appears to resolve all these conflicts and similarities into the one symbol.

> Labour is blossoming or dancing where
> The body is not bruised to pleasure soul,
> Nor beauty born out of its own despair,
> Nor blear-eyed wisdom out of midnight oil.
> O chestnut tree, great-rooted blossomer,
> Are you the leaf, the blossom, or the bole ?
> O body swayed to music, O brightening glance,
> How can we know the dancer from the dance ?

Thus *Among School Children* presents references to myths and beliefs that are basic to two great civilizations, perceives similarity and dissimilarity. and discovers one symbol which brings all things into unity.

The interpretation of this one symbol has caused a good deal of head-scratching and I am happy not to have to go into it at all thoroughly. I wish only to relate it, and the poem in which it appears, to the series of other autobiographical meditations which Yeats composed, and this but briefly. The poem *All Souls' Night* is one of this series, and again presents many images which the poet wishes to contemplate, 'Till meditation master all its parts'. In *The Winding Stair and Other Poems* (1933) *A Dialogue of Self and Soul* performs the same manoeuvre. Here the speaker states

> I am content to follow to its source
> Every event in action or in thought;
> Measure the lot; . . .

In *Blood and the Moon* the speaker sees his 'ancestral stair' as one travelled by Goldsmith, Berkeley, Burke, and Swift, and relates it to the dead civilizations of Alexandria and Babylon. The non-autobiographical

The Seven Sages deals also with the Irish Tradition and makes use of the same characters. *Coole Park, 1929* and *Coole Park and Ballylee, 1931*, again autobiographical meditations, discuss the traditions of poetry and scholarship, and their 'Traditional sanctity and loveliness'. *Vacillation* relates philosophies of different cultures and focuses them through the lens of the one inquiring contemplative mind. In *A Full Moon in March* (1935), *Parnell's Funeral* relates present-day Ireland to the Ireland of Swift and to images of ancient Sicily and Crete. In the *Last Poems* (1939) the syncretic tendency is observable in numerous poems—*An Acre of Grass* places Shakespeare and Blake alongside Michelangelo; *The Municipal Gallery Revisited* repeats the manoeuvres of the Coole Park poems. *The Statues* develops its theme with reference to Greek Civilization, the Middle Ages, Shakespeare, Irish Legend, and the Easter Rising of 1916. *Long-Legged Fly* sees Julius Caesar, Helen of Troy, a child in a street, and Michelangelo as illustrative of the same principle. *The Circus Animals' Desertion*, more narrowly autobiographical than many, nevertheless is in the same series as the Coole poems. It is in *Lapis Lazuli*, however, that the syncretic, or synoptic method reaches a new clarity. The first paragraph refers to the poets as being 'gay' and contrives to mention both King Billy and the zeppelin raids of the First World War. The second paragraph deals with Shakespearean tragedy and maintains that 'Hamlet and Lear are gay', suggesting that there is a triumphant gaiety in the way the poet has mastered and understood his themes of human agony. The third paragraph presents us with an image of the fall of civilizations under the attack of wandering hordes, and points out that Callimachus's sculpture is now totally lost. Here however we are made to see the poet's gaiety in a new light:

> No handiwork of Callimachus,
> Who handled marble as if it were bronze,
> Made draperies that seemed to rise
> When sea-wind swept the corner, stands;
> His long lamp-chimney shaped like the stem
> Of a slender palm, stood but a day;
> All things fall and are built again,
> And those that build them again are gay.

This is the poet's duty, and justification. He is not simply the self-reflecting creator of a hall of mirrors, but a continual renewer of past achievements, a living embodiment of tradition. Tradition, in the last verse paragraph of the poem, is presented to us by way of three Chinamen carved in lapis lazuli, who stare 'on all the tragic scene'

> One asks for mournful melodies;
> Accomplished fingers begin to play.
> Their eyes mid many wrinkles, their eyes,
> Their ancient, glittering eyes, are gay.

The role of the poet, therefore, is twofold. He must bring all things into unity, the past into unity with the present, the Classical with the Christian, the nationalist with the cosmic, the local with the general; and he must remake what has fallen, thus becoming at once the worker in many traditions, and the unifier of all.

This view of the poet's function successfully answers the problem of Authority posed at the beginning of this chapter. It does not, however, solve the question of the means towards this end. The means Yeats chose were as various as the task demanded. He wrote ballads in which his sense of the vulgar tradition was fused with his appreciation of its essential dignity. His mixed diction gave his ballads the same balance of formality and freedom which one finds in the Border Ballads, without in any way imitating them. He adopted the tone of the lyric poet desired by Synge, making poems which were simultaneously earthy and controlled. He developed the eclogue form and the poetic-sequence. Where his own central *persona* (that of the all-combining Maker) was too myriad-minded for his matter he took on the mask of Crazy Jane, or Tom of Cruachan, or of an anonymous Man or Woman, or of a Saint, or Ballad singer. In each poem he presented sharp conflicts, dramatic assertions, vivid paradoxes, which can all be found restated, and resolved, in the great series of meditations where the brooding mind of the Master-Poet, the 'great dancer', shows itself conscious of its 'own life and the dance'. As a consequence, the viewpoints expressed in the different poems are not consistent with one another. Judicious selection will result in one's tracing Yeats's debt to this or that tradition; one can make him out as essentially a Neo-Platonist, or an Irish Nationalist, or a sophisticated folk-poet, or a fascist, or a solipsist, or almost what one wishes. Much, of course, can be made to fit with Neo-Platonism for that is a philosophic system which is itself syncretic, bringing many strangers into companionship with an Elizabethan dexterity and capacity for double-think.

There is, however, one central symbol, one unifying force, and this is the fully achieved *persona* of the Master-Poet which contains all human attitudes and passions. Yeats's autobiographical meditations are so contrived as to relate together, in personal terms, many widely differing attitudes, with each of which he shows sympathy for one reason or another. Lady Gregory, Synge, Horton, The Middletons, Pollexfens, Dowson, Johnson, Robert Gregory, Hugh Lane, Daniel O'Leary, would probably agree with one another on no single point were they to be placed in the same room. Grattan, Swift, Burke, Goldsmith, and Berkeley would make a somewhat lively committee. Blake and Plotinus might agree on occasion, but what of Aristotle, Michelangelo, Sato, Landor, Donne, and that fisherman in Connemara tweeds? The only conceivable meeting place is the mind of Yeats, a mind of Shakespearean capacity.

It is not its capacity, however, which is its most astonishing characteristic: it is its ability to so order its contents as to give us the impression that it is an embodiment of a whole culture. The references combine to remind us that the Master-Poet is a man representative of all European cultural history. Sometimes they indicate, more narrowly, his being representative of the culture and history of Ireland; but even when this is the case the masterful references to Irish phenomena as being significant of universal principles and traditions make us see Ireland as itself a summary of human experience and human history. References to Greek Philosophy, and to Medieval Art, both unify and universalize his meditations by relating them to cultural fundamentals of Western Civilization.

In this Yeats is doing neither more nor less than the Master-Poets who preceded him. If we look at the work of Dante, Chaucer, Spenser, Ben Jonson, and Milton we see that each attempted to fuse together different traditions, to marry the 'Classical' with his national inheritance, to comment upon the role of the poet even as he performed it, and to produce work which could be viewed as emanating from a mind and sensibility representative of the central beliefs and concerns of Western Civilization. Later poets did much the same, though, as it became increasingly more difficult and finally impossible for one man to have even a smattering of all existing knowledge in history, philosophy and literature, the master-works became more limited in range. Thus, in the Romantic period, Wordsworth's major work was an autobiographical investigation of poetry and the mind of the poet, Byron's masterpiece was wider ranging but avoided the darker depths, and Tennyson's *Idylls of the King* was a narrowly national epic. Whitman in his *Leaves of Grass* chose to characterize and embody a national sensibility and suggest that it was central to all humanity and Browning chose to create in terms of a version of medieval Italy which gave him the opportunity to explore what he clearly felt to be a significant cultural crux and matrix.

Pound, a follower of both Browning and Whitman, attempted the larger scope of a truly international poem, a universal contemplation of the lot of man. All these poets, however, like Yeats, took synopsis, syncresis and synthesis as their three guiding principles, and all, for better or worse, gave poetry a new Authority in their time.

NINE A Way of Life

Only a very small number of poets in any given period even begin to approach the Master-Poet status which W. B. Yeats achieved. The majority of poets cannot control their sensibilities to the extent required to enable them to synthesize personal and learned experience into a 'poetic personality' that can speak with authority and present a universal vision. Indeed, the poet very often loses control of his imagination, and faces a confusion of stimuli with which he cannot cope. This loss of control is attributable to several causes. Firstly, it must be obvious by now that the twentieth-century poet has so many 'styles' and 'modes' available to him that it is hard for him to select the one mode within which he can fulfil his potential most easily. He is liable to thresh around, advancing, retreating, experimenting, until he falls victim to the most intense kind of frustration. In addition to this, the poet in this century has no single philosophic tradition to enable him to see a pattern in his experience. He cannot, like Dante, explore in terms of Christianity. He cannot even, like Pope, explore within the confines of a generally accepted view of the nature of society and the poet's role within it. He is obliged all too often to attempt to create or discover a world-view of his own. This is difficult for him as he is likely (as Keats pointed out) to be by nature unable to achieve fixed opinions, and temperamentally opposed to the rigidities of systematized thought. If he is fortunate enough to be brought up within a particular religious or philosophical tradition he can work in terms of it, even though his work may seem to rebel against it. If he has no orthodoxy against which or within which to work he may either find himself unable to order his poetic discoveries into an authoritative system or retreat into the writing of mere social comment. Kathleen Raine commented:

> Joyce did not perhaps belong to an orthodoxy, but he was *related* to an orthodoxy in his work. If you are not related to an orthodoxy you are in danger of sinking into the journalistic norm or the popular norm, which is not good enough. Perhaps we have to belong, not only to a single orthodoxy, but to the total orthodoxy of man's aspiration, which

is the Perennial Philosophy as a whole. The one orthodoxy, the orthodoxy of all orthodoxies; many would say that in some respects Christianity is a deviation: I'm a Platonist myself, and that, after all, has been the real religion of Western Art, hasn't it? In other times, clearly, Christianity provided a common frame of reference to which poets could align themselves and be understood by their readers. . . .

But I come more and more to see that the real orthodoxy, the real religion of European Art—it goes right back—is Neo-Platonism. It comes up again and again. It's a secret language of the poets. I have learned immeasurably from it. I don't think one can go, as the young are going, to India, and use ideas derived from India untranslated into European terms. But there have been renewals through an intake of some foreign culture at all times; whether India will be digestible in this sense remains to be seen. I hope it will be so.

A large number of contemporary poets have attempted to relate to the orthodoxies of the East, particularly to Zen Buddhism. Many American poets, like Cid Corman and Gary Snyder, have developed a profound understanding of Zen and this has enabled them to develop poetic explorations of real importance. Other poets have attempted to relate to different systems of thought and speculation. Robert Graves has devoted much attention to Sufism, though only a poet of Graves' strength could, I think, derive much support from a religious philosophy so splendidly free of the comforting formulae of dogma and ritual. Many poets have found the Catholic Church of help to them, though few of these could be described as orthodox Catholics or even practising ones, in the Church's terms.

All men, perhaps, need a philosophy of life to support them and to help them to make sense of their experiences. It would be unwise to claim that the need of poets is more desperate than that of anyone else. Nevertheless the poet does start with a disadvantage. He is a sensitive; he lacks one layer of skin; he registers more intensely than most. Theodore Roethke wrote in a notebook of 1943–47:[1]

The feeling that one is on the edge of many things: that there are many worlds from which we are separated by only a film; that a flick of the wrist, a turn of the body another way will bring us to a new world. It is more than a perpetual expectation: yet sometimes the sense of richness is haunting: it is richness and yet denial, this living a half a step,

[1] This, and all subsequent quotations from Theodore Roethke's notebooks, are taken from David Wagoner (ed.), *Straw for the Fire: from the Notebooks of Theodore Roethke, 1943–1963*. Doubleday 1972.

as it were, from what one should be. The valleys are always green, but only the eyes, never the feet, are there . . . The feeling is always with us. . . .

In another part of the same notebook he wrote:

At that time the significance of small acts . . . even an old carpet was a dazzle of scenes, and the clock never told me more; a turn of the head a panorama of difference.

And in another place:

How terrible the need for God.

Edwin Muir was once obliged by circumstance to work as a clerk in a bone-processing factory in Fairport. Although he himself was not required to handle the decaying, stinking raw material, he reported later, 'I could not stave off a feeling of degradation'. He suggests in his autobiography that it was this environment which led him to experience a 'blind inward unhappiness'. He wrote in his Autobiography:[1]

During my years in Fairport. . . . I had experienced now and then an anxious vague dread which I could not explain or attach to any object. Its real cause, I feel pretty certain, was my work in the bone-yard. This state now grew worse, or I became more conscious of it, realizing that it was bound up with my feeling of separation and yearning. Standing before a shop-window, or taking a country walk, I would waken with a start, conscious that for some time, I had been staring at some chance object, a ring in a jeweller's shop, or a hill in the distance, with a dry, defeated longing. It was as if I could grasp what was before my eyes only by an enormous effort, and even then an invisible barrier, a wall of distance, separated me from it. I moved in a crystalline globe or bubble, insulated from the life around me, yet filled with desire to reach it, to be at the very heart of it and lose myself there. I was most subject to this state when I was by myself, but I sometimes felt it when I was with other people, so that my absent-mindedness became fantastic, and my friends, when they were out with me, would look round anxiously, as if they were afraid I would get lost. My state made me seek company with desperate eagerness; I was more sociable and more lonely than I had ever been before. I often woke in the night with this feeling of mingled longing and dread, and when I began to read Dante much later and came to the passage describing the souls approaching the river of Acheron I recognized my own state:

[1] Edwin Muir, op. cit., pp. 149–150.

e pronti sono a trapassar lo rio,
che la divina giustizia li sprona
sì, che la tema si volge in dislò.

'And they are quick to cross the river, for Divine Justice spurs them
on, so that dread is transformed to longing.' But in my case it was
longing that seemed to be transformed to dread: I stared at things for
which I did not care a farthing, as if I wanted to attach myself to them
for ever, to lose myself in a hill or a tiny gewgaw in a shop window,
creep into it, and be secure there. But at the same time dread raised
its walls round me, cutting me off; for even while I yearned for these
things I felt a hidden menace in them, so that the simplest object was
dangerous and might destroy me. A memory of this state returns
whenever I read Wordsworth's lines in *The Affliction of Margaret*:

> My apprehensions come in crowds;
> I dread the rustling of the grass;
> The very shadows of the clouds
> Have power to shake me as they pass.

A jagged stone or a thistle seemed to be bursting with malice, as if
they had been put in the world to cut and gash; the dashing of break-
ers on rocks terrified me, for I was both the wave and the rock; it was
as though I were both too close to things and immeasurably distant from
them.

This experience is clearly close to that of Roethke; both poets felt 'a
perpetual expectation', and were aware of being separated by only a thin
film from some other world of experience. Muir's state of anxiety and
dread continued after he married and left Fairport for London. It led
him into a series of waking dreams or visions which later provided him
with much of the symbolism of his poetry. He was at this time in the
care of an analyst. He had not been dreaming (or aware of dreaming)
for some time, but now 'dreams came in crowds'. One of those dreams,
together with his analyst's reaction to it, is worth giving in detail.
Muir wrote:[1]

One evening after working in the office I came back at six o'clock
feeling ill. I lay down on the couch in the sitting-room with my face
to the wall. Willa was sitting at the table behind me, correcting
examination papers for the cramming college; I listened to the sheets
rustling as she turned them over, and they seemed to make a curiously
loud noise in the room. Then my breathing too grew louder and—

[1] ibid., pp. 159–163.

this is the only way in which I can describe it—deliberate at the same time, as if I were breathing because I had willed it, not because I could not help it: the first act or rehearsal of breath. I felt my breast rising and falling, and something pressing upon it, which I flung off and drew back again. This turned into a great dark blue wave of sea-water, advancing and receding. A dark blue seascape opened on the lighted wall before me, a dark blue sky arched over it; and as if I had slipped out of my body I was standing on the shore looking at the waves rolling in. A little distance out a naked woman was posted; the waves dashed against her, washing up to her breasts and falling again; but she never moved; she seemed to be fixed there like a statue rising out of some other dimension. Then everything vanished and I was at the bottom of the sea, with the waves far above me. When I came up again—all this time I was lying on the couch listening to the rustling of the papers behind me—the sea and the sky were perfectly white like paper; in the distance some black jagged rocks stuck out of the stagnant water; there was no colour anywhere but black and white. I began to swim at a great speed (at this time I had not yet learned to swim) towards the nearest rock. Round me countless creatures were circling and diving, glass-coloured in the white sea: long cylinders about the length of a man, without head or tails, mouths or eyes. I reached the rock and put out my hand to draw myself up, when one of these creatures fixed itself by the upper end, which seemed to have a little sucker, to the middle of my brow just above my eyes. Filled with rage, I kicked the creature with my bare toes; at last I kicked it through, and it fell like a broken bottle into the sea. All this time I had no fear. I pulled myself to the top of the rock.

After this my memory of the dream is fragmentary for a while. I think that it must have been an unbroken sequence, but the pictures followed one another at such a speed that I could not catch all of them. What I remember next is wandering through a rough woodland country interspersed with little brown rocks, where there were troops of low-browed, golden-haired, silent creatures somewhat like monkeys, while I saw in the distance a procession of white-robed female figures slowly passing as if to silent music. I wandered there, it seemed to me, for a long time. I remember coming to what I thought was the green, mossy trunk of a fallen tree; as I looked at it I saw that it was a dragon, and that it was slowly weeping its eyes into a little heap before it: the eyes were like brooches, ringed blue and red and white, hard and enamelled so that they tinkled as they fell. All this seemed natural to me; each pair of eyes as they fell appearing to be pushed out by other eyes behind them. Here there was another break in the dream. The next scene was quite different. I was in a wild, rocky place, treeless and shrubless, and in the middle of it I came to an enormous white palace. The walls

were high and windowless, and there was only one small door. I went
up to it and pushed. The door opened at once, but when I took my
hand away shut again, and would not open a second time. Then I saw
a small opening, about three feet square, just beside the door. Creeping
through it, I stepped on to the balcony of a great hall. Looking up, I
could see the roof far above me; but downward the hall went farther
than my eyes could follow, and seemed to sink deep into the ground.
This lower part was covered with wooden scaffoldings, and was
obviously under repair, though no workmen could be seen; the place
seemed to have been deserted for a long time. I climbed on to the
balustrade, raised my hands above my head, and dived. I had fallen
head downward for a great distance, when my hand caught a beam of
one of the scaffoldings, and I began to climb upward again, hand over
hand, at a great speed, with the ease of an ape. I did not stop until my
head was touching the ceiling and I could go no farther. Again I was
filled with rage, I beat my head against the ceiling, which was thick
and decorated with fine mouldings, and broke through it. Above,
there was a broad terrace lined with cypresses; night had fallen, and
the dark blue sky was glittering with stars. Tall, robed men were
walking with melodramatic stateliness along the terrace, under the
trees.

There was another break here, and when I caught the dream again
I was standing beside a little mountain pool fringed with rushes. The
sky had the whitish bruised look which it sometimes has before sun-
rise. As I looked at it I saw two little clouds like scraps of paper slowly
floating towards each other, and for the first time I was afraid, I could
not tell why. The two clouds met, blazed up, and turned into an angry
sun. The sun began to revolve across the sky. As it revolved two serpents, one red and the other yellow, broke through its crust and began
a furious locked battle. Still revolving, bearing the battling serpents
with it, the sun burst into flames and in a moment turned to ashes.
Black now, it went on wheeling across the paper-white sky. Then it
stopped; its periphery trembled and quivered, and I saw that it was
legged like a centipede. It began to come down diagonally towards
me, walking on an invisible thread like a spider. As it came near I
saw that it was a fabulous creature with an armoured body and a head
somewhat like the prow of a sailing-ship, the head being partly that
of a woman and partly that of a bird. Its body was jointed in the middle,
and looked like two enormous tortoises one on top of the other. I saw
now that I was naked and holding a broad sword in my hands. I lifted
up the sword, swung it over my shoulder, and struck the creature on
the brow. The blow made no alteration. I raised the sword again and
struck harder, but the stroke merely pushed the head back. In a fury,
I thrust the sword into the beast's side at the joint of the armour; then

it turned its head and *smiled* at me. This inflamed my fury past all bounds; I twisted the sword round and round; the mail burst open; something with white wings robed in white, fluttered into the sky; and the creature drew its torn mail round it like an umbrella shutting, thrusting its beak into the ground, and shot out of sight.

I think there was another break here, though not a long one. The next I remember is seeing countless angels flying high up in the air, going through absurd and lovely evolutions, looping the loop, hiding behind the edges of clouds: the whole sky was filled with them. I watched an ordered formation of them flying over a still stretch of water, so that I could see them reflected in it as they passed above me in their flight. Then I was in the air, and when I was a little distance up some one took my hand; it was my wife. We flew up, now and then dropping extravagant curtsies to each other in the air, with a wide and light sweep, keeping our wings still. After a while I noticed that the wing on the shoulder next to her had fallen off, and looking at her I saw that the wing on her corresponding shoulder had disappeared too, so that we were mounting the air on two wings. After we had flown like this for a while we looked down and saw a great crowd ranged in concentric rings beneath us, and in the middle of it a gigantic figure clad in antique armour, sitting on a throne with a naked sword at his side. We flew down and settled on his shoulders, and bending behind his neck kissed each other.

When this waking dream, or trance, or vision ended I was quite well; all my sickness had gone. I astonished Willa by telling her about it; we discussed it for a long time, and then I wrote it down in my note-book along with my other dreams. Next day was the day for seeing my analyst; I handed the notebook to him, and there was a long silence. At last I asked him what he made of the dream, and told him that I had been awake the whole time, conscious of the light of the lamp and the rustling of the papers behind me. He said something about its being a myth of the creation, and warned me that my unconscious was far too near the surface for my comfort and safety, and that I should hurry to put something substantial between myself and it. The advice seemed sensible, but not of the slightest use to me; I knew of no substance which I could suddenly improvise as a buffer against myself; I might as well have been told to add a cubit to my stature.

Other waking dreams followed. Muir wrote:[1]

All these waking dreams I took to my analyst, who was now growing concerned about me. I told him again that I could let them go on or stop them, and asked him what he advised me to do. He strongly

[1] ibid., p. 165.

advised me to stop them. I did as he bade me, and my waking dreams ceased at once, and have never come back again. I doubt now whether I was right in stopping them; I feel that if I had let these visions continue they would have ceased at their own time, instead of at mine. On the other hand, I may have been too close at this stage to the borderline between sanity and insanity; but I do not for a moment believe it. The analyst was concerned for the health of my mind, he was trying to bring me back to normality, whatever that is, and I do not see what other advice he could have given me.

Muir's problems certainly arose in part from the psychological damage inflicted upon him by his experiences in Glasgow and in the Fairport bone-processing factory, as well as earlier experiences of intense poverty, and of the painful illnesses and early deaths of his father, mother, and two brothers. It may be that conscious life had become so painful to him that he could only turn to the more vivid, even if often terrifying, visions of the unconscious.

Jeni Couzyn, discussing the predicament of the poet troubled by hypersensitivity, said:

> People who can write poems, or who want to write poems, are people who don't have walls. I've got a poem in my book *Flying* about that, called *A Lady of Pain* and it says
>
> > she was a lady without walls.
> > In her body
> > there were many cells, each
> > vulnerable to the currents of the city
> > and the seasons and the planets.
>
> Without walls you feel physically, through the cells, something beyond the immediate physical reality. And I think that these walls are broken down in our society by pain, so that very often people with an unhappy childhood turn out to be like that. But on the other hand I think that in a far more civilized society than ours people would be able to dispense with walls altogether. What I mean is that poets are exceptional because they don't have those walls. They don't have the protection and the blindness that the walls offer. But you need blindness to survive in our society. If you don't have it, then you write poems and you suffer and everything. But in a proper civilization human beings wouldn't need those walls at all. . .
>
> *You are almost approaching Plato who said that Poets weren't necessary in the Ideal State.*
>
> Well, I think that everybody is a poet and everybody should be a

poet, and that poets should be the exception is just a barometer of the sickness of our society . . . I mean that the damaging, harassing, battering of our society is what makes people need to put up those protective walls. Those truths that are underneath or beyond or outside—people who haven't got those walls can hear and see and feel. What happens is that you are born without the walls; you are born in direct touch with what I call the Ocean, and that gradually a normal good upbringing teaches you how to build those walls.

Which means that you don't think a normal good upbringing is good or should be normal

That's right! Well it can't be because a normal good upbringing is something that's teaching you how to cope with the most disgusting, stressful, abnormal situation. If you learn well, then you learn how to protect yourself, and poets are people who have learned badly. It's perhaps dangerous to make these generalizations, but every poet I know is someone who has been shattered in some way—usually early. I was listening to a bunch of actors and actresses talking one time, and they were all saying that their childhood had had an absence of love. I thought 'Ah, they are compensating for this absence in the public nature of their work.' It's not quite the same with poets. I don't think they've had an absence of love necessarily; rather some very extreme kind of battering.

The portrait of the poet as a person 'without walls', one who has not learned to protect himself, and therefore one who is always in danger of falling victim to the pressures of society and to the intensity of his own perceptions is one that we must examine further. Certainly, many poets have had periods of madness or severe emotional disturbance. The roll-call is frightening, for it includes some of the most impressive poets we have had, including Christopher Smart, John Clare, William Cowper, Jonathan Swift, Thomas L. Beddoes, and, in our own century, we know that severe mental breakdowns have been suffered by David Gascoyne, Robert Lowell, Theodore Roethke, Sylvia Plath, and John Berryman among others. The list of suicides is also troubling, for it includes, in our own time, Weldon Kees, Sylvia Plath, Randal Jarrell, and John Berryman, all poets of intense sensibility and power. It is no secret that there are many alcoholics among the poets: Dylan Thomas is not the only poet of stature to have destroyed himself with alcohol, and I could, were I inclined, list the names of over a score of living poets of real quality who have what is currently known as 'a bottle problem'. Lawrence Durrell said in *The Red Limbo Lingo* 'The alcoholism of poets may be explained thus—they have seen the full horror of the human predicament.'[1] John Gawsworth's route to destruction was whisky. He had, as a young man, achieved a deserved reputation as a bibliographer. After the Second World War, however, his drinking led to his becoming unemployable. G. S. Fraser said of him

> Gawsworth had many friends who tried to help him, but he had a talent for disaster. Since he had no fixed abode, he could not draw national assistance; his friends started a fund for him but, when he could lay his hands on any of this, it went on whisky, and whisky took him to hospital. Behind this self-destructive drive there was, I think, a feeling that as a poet he was utterly forgotten and perhaps, he may have felt in his inner heart, deservedly so.[2]

Gawsworth was defeated by that fear of failure which so often attends the poets, and in his case (for his later poetry did not bear out the promise of his earlier) the fear was justified. It must be understood that this fear of failure is not quite the same as the fear of the merchant, the banker, the athlete even. It is fear that one has lost touch with all that makes life worth living. It is ultimate desolation. Theodore Roethke pointed to the intensity of the poet's desire to *be* a poet, to remain in touch with the Daimon, when he wrote:

> In my poems there is much more reality than in any relationship or affection that I feel; when I create, I am true, and I would like to find the strength to base my life entirely on this truth, on this infinite simplicity and joy. . . .

Gawsworth, like so many others, lost that truth and joy, and the knowledge of that loss destroyed him. General awareness of the incidence of insanity, suicide, and alcoholism among the poets has led recently to some writers treating these subjects with a kind of admiring romanticism. Poets are praised for having had the courage to advance right to the edge of sanity in the pursuit of their vision. They should be honoured for taking risks with their emotional lives in order to provide us with insights that others have shied away from. There is some truth in this. The poet who continually and persistently attempts to explore the darker portions of the human psyche, who deliberately, like Rimbaud, disorders his mind in order to perceive what the ordered, and safely enclosed, mind cannot perceive, is taking risks. We must, however, realize that the poet may not be able to help taking these risks; he may, because of his lack of

[1] Lawrence Durrell, *The Red Limbo Lingo*. Faber 1971, p. 15.
[2] G. S. Fraser, *Lawrence Durrell, A Study*. Faber 1968, p. 19.

'walls', find it impossible to avoid danger without denying his vocation absolutely and refusing to listen to that inner voice which is his Daimon, even though he knows that this may lead him into periods of hallucination and, perhaps, paranoia, or an intensity of perception which sends him out of control. Theodore Roethke told Allan Seager of one occasion when intensity of feeling led him to lose control.

> For no reason I started to feel very good. Suddenly I knew how to enter into the life of everything around me. I knew how it felt to be a tree, a blade of grass, even a rabbit. I didn't sleep much. I just walked around with this wonderful feeling. One day I was passing a diner and all of a sudden I knew what it felt to be a lion. I went into the diner and said to the counterman, 'Bring me a steak. Don't cook it. Just bring it.' So he brought me this raw steak and I started eating it. The other customers made like they were revolted, watching me. And I began to see that maybe it *was* a little strange. So I went to the Dean and said, 'I feel too good. Get me down off this.' So they put me into the tubs.[1]

Seager tells us that

> After he had married he told his wife that this first episode had been self-induced 'to reach a new level of reality.' Both Peter De Vries and John Clark, as they looked back on it, felt the same thing. There seemed to have been a deliberateness in his behaviour that autumn, and his drinking and pill taking seemed to have a purpose. Perhaps he was trying an experiment in his classes but he did not say what it was or why he needed a new emotional thrust to make it. Later, at Penn State, in conversation with William Haag, he mentioned Rimbaud's 'dérèglement de tous les sens' approvingly, saying it was one way of breaking out of one's self, but at this time, at Michigan State, it is doubtful if he had read Rimbaud.
>
> He had many later episodes and under treatment, he was diagnosed by his psychiatrists as a 'manic-depressive neurotic, but not typical', and as a 'paranoid schizophrenic'. Each of the psychiatrists told me that one of the characteristics of manic-depressive patients was their insistence that they brought their attacks on themselves.
>
> The actual causes of these states are unknown. A few years ago psychiatrists attributed them to purely psychic traumata, often occurring very early in life. Now there is a tendency to view them as biological, possibly enzyme changes in the nervous system, but nothing is definitely known. It is also possible that a patient's environment, if

[1] Allan Seager, *The Glass House: The Life of Theodore Roethke*, McGraw Hill 1968, p. 101.

it seems unfavourable, may exert a pressure on him and that this pressure may institute biological changes that cause an episode.[1]

Seager comments further on Roethke's condition in an appendix to his biography. He writes:

> In a recent book, *Positive Disintegration* (Little, Brown, 1964), the Polish psychiatrist, Casimierz Dabrowski, against the teaching of Freud and his followers, argues that some neuroses, even psychoses, may be benign. Personality, Dabrowski says, develops primarily through dissatisfaction with and the fragmentation of one's existing psychic structure. Stimulated by a lack of harmony in the self and in adaptation to the strains of the external environment, the individual 'disintegrates'. Anxiety, neurosis, psychosis may be *symptoms* of the disintegration and they mark a retrogression to a lower level of psychic functioning. Finally reintegration occurs at a higher level and the personality evolves to a new plateau of psychic health. Dabrowski points out that these new integrations at 'higher' levels seem to happen to people of high intelligence and marked creative powers.
>
> Thus the Albany episode might be regarded not as an interruption in his life but perhaps as a spur to a new psychic synthesis of Ted's creative energies that enabled him to push forward and break new ground in his work.[2]

Stephen Spender commented on Roethke

> Entering into his work—indeed becoming it—his world *là-bas* where words become loam and roots and snails and slugs lying along some bright chips of jangles from nursery rhymes and gashed childhood memories—Roethke is forever on the edge of Rimbaud's goal of the systematic *dérèglement de tous les sens*. One does not know whether to rejoice with the poems or sympathize with the poet; for the disintegration which bore strange and marvellous fruit in his poetry caused tragic breakdowns in his life.[3]

Dr William Hoffer, one of Roethke's psychiatrists, told Seager, 'I think his troubles were merely the running expenses he paid for being his kind of poet'.[4] Beatrice Roethke told Seager, 'When Ted and I were first married he thought it (mental illness) might be a requisite, but over a period of years he revised his thinking about this, I believe. What are generally thought of as his best poems were written when he was well and out of the hospital.'[5]

From all this we might reasonably deduce that the poet's breakdowns

[1] ibid., pp. 101–102.   [2] ibid., pp. 278–288.   [3] ibid., p. 289.
[4] ibid., p. 109.   [5] ibid., p. 290.

may be the direct consequence of pushing intense awareness to its limits or they may be the consequence of the poet's being obliged to operate within an oppressive or anti-poetic environment, and that both these factors may well be involved in any given instance.

Roethke's notebooks contain a number of passages which relate to this matter.

The true way is close, just as the remove from madness is close.

* * *

A poem that is the shape of the psyche itself; in times of great stress that's what I tried to write

* * *

Give me the madman's sudden insight and the child's spiritual dignity.

* * *

Those who are willing to be vulnerable move among mysteries.

* * *

There comes a time in the poet's life when one personality even with several sides is not enough. Then he can either go mad or become a dramatist.

* * *

God robbed poets of their minds that they might be made expressions of his own.

* * *

Always basing my life on the intangible, the impossible.

* * *

It's the poet's business to be more, not less, than a man.

* * *

Many meditations destroy.

Roethke himself has described how his breakdowns sometimes came hard upon a time of intense perception. Mrs Randall Jarrell wrote of her husband in 1963[1]

Randall's nervous breakdown was showing signs that all but we could see. Before the worst of it happened, he was granted a few magic weeks of Lisztian virtuosity when nothing in his lectures or reading was veiled to him any longer. Everything his heart desired seemed possible to him. (He even met and *talked* to Unitas one day—and wrote a poem about it the next.) Poems flew at him, short ones, quatrains,

[1] Robert Lowell, Peter Taylor, and Robert Penn Warren (eds.), *Randall Jarrell 1914–1965*. Farrar, Straus and Geroux 1967, p. 297.

182

haiku, aphorisms, parts of poems, ideas for poems until just words beat at his head like many wings. Before it was through with us, this ordeal called forth a desperate valor we'd never have known we had; and Donne's lines '. . . for affliction is a treasure, and scarce any man hath enough of it . . . that is not . . . ripened by it and made fit for God . . .' came to have more meaning for us than I'd have wished.

The burst of creative energy which preceded Jarrell's breakdown is not uncommon. It is as if the poet, caught up entirely in his vision, becomes possessed by it. It is, one might almost say, Daimonic possession; the Daimon who should be guide becomes despot. In discussing Hölderlin's insanity Michael Hamburger says:[1]

> The mental disorder which undermined Hölderlin's intellect was schizophrenia, or dementia praecox, as it used to be called. He had always had the disposition of a schizophrenic, but in the thirty-sixth year of his life the disease became acute and permanent. Professor C. G. Jung gives an explanation of this form of insanity: Just as one person can disappear in a social role, so another can vanish in an inner vision and be lost in his environment because of it. Many incomprehensible changes in the personality such as sudden conversions or other deep-seated transformations originate in the mysterious, attractive power of a collective image, which . . . can cause such a degree of inflation that the whole personality may be dissolved. This dissolution means insanity, either transitory or permanent, a 'splitting of the mind', or schizophrenia.

Hamburger refers to Karl Jaspers.[2]

> Prof. Karl Jaspers, in his book on Strindberg and van Gogh, deals with Hölderlin's illness as well as more recent discoveries about schizophrenia permit. Above all, he does not try to depreciate or explain away the singular beauty of Hölderlin's mature poetry by calling it the product of an insane mind: 'In the same way as a diseased oyster causes pearls to form, schizophrenic processes can allow unique spiritual works to be formed. And those who experience the power of works which for them, generate life, do not think of schizophrenia, which may have been one of the conditions of their creation, any more than the person who derives pleasure from the pearl thinks of the oyster's disease. But those who desire understanding enquire into origins and circumstances, and no limit can be set to their enquiries. The fact is that no pathological inquest can help us to understand

---

[1] Michael Hamburger, *Hölderlin*. Harvill Press 1942, pp. 71–72.
[2] ibid., pp. 72–73.

Hölderlin's poetry, as Prof. Jaspers pointed out: 'At present, psychiatry possesses categories which are much too crude to allow us to analyse Hölderlin's poetry written in the first years of schizophrenia by means of these categories.'

All that can be determined is that Hölderlin was schizophrenic, that his poetry was influenced by this disposition, and that, as Prof. Jaspers shows, he had something in common with other schizophrenics: 'It has been observed how schizophrenics form their own mythology, which for them exists self-evidently and unquestionably, and which often adopts this timeless quality. The contents of dreams, these products of schizophrenia, and the myths provided by history have been well compared and significant parallels have been discovered.' This takes us back to Jung's theory of the 'collective unconscious', according to which Hölderlin was one of the most thorough and penetrating explorers of all time.

Schizophrenia is the label that has been used to describe the condition of a number of poets who have suffered breakdowns. Another term used has been Paranoia. It is characteristic of the paranoid that everything he reads, experiences, or perceives, is made by him to serve as evidence and proof of his overmastering delusion. Salvador Dali has used the term *Paranoia* to describe art for this reason; everything the artist (or poet) comes across becomes, when he is in his most creative state, grist for his mill. Everything supports and tends to prove the truth and reality of his world-view, his myth, his pattern of the universe. Pound's condition of mind in 1946, after he had been through the hell of the prisoner's cage at Pisa, was described by Dr Marion King, who was then medical director of the United States Public Health Service, as 'a paranoid state'. His description of Pound's behaviour at that time, however, may remind one of that manic condition of extreme creative confidence which we have already noticed in others. Dr King said in his report of 14 December 1945, 'He is abnormally grandiose, is expansive and exuberant in manner, exhibiting pressure of speech, discursiveness, and distractibility'.[1]

The cases of Roethke, Jarrell, and Pound all show an excess of energy, a storm of psychic energy, as characteristic of the breakdown. This phenomenon has been observed in a number of other cases known to me but which I do not feel it proper to discuss by name. In one instance the poet became convinced he was either Christ or a messenger of Christ with a great truth to tell the Head of State. He was caught attempting,

[1] William Van O'Connor and Edward Stone (eds.), *A Casebook on Ezra Pound.* Thomas Y Crowell Company 1959, p. 25.

while not fully dressed, to get into the Head of State's residence. In other cases the energy appears to be directed negatively rather than positively: instead of experiencing intense euphoria and creativity the poet suffers the blackest and most total despair. His work is useless. He can no longer write. His vision has been false, or else it would have brought him fame or at least inner certainty. All his powers are now directed deathward, and, in such a condition, he may attempt suicide.

I have painted a dark picture of the poets and their risks by discussing cases which might reasonably be regarded as extreme. Other poets have had less intense experiences of breakdown, and some have escaped almost entirely. T. S. Eliot wrote the greater part of *The Waste Land* while in a sanatorium in Lausanne suffering from intense nervous and emotional exhaustion. His condition, however, seems to have been caused largely by the difficulties of his personal domestic life rather than by the demands made upon him by his poetry, though it would seem sensible to believe that his poetic vocation cannot have helped him towards that self-protective insensitivity which his situation demanded. Edwin Muir, afflicted very much by the pressures of his environment, became deeply depressed, but the psychotherapy he received appears to have been one of the chief agents in the flowering of his poetic vision and to have been responsible for his coming to terms with the archetypal images which haunted his dreams and disturbed his days. Other poets have had periods of depression and emotional disturbance of varying degrees of intensity, and in some cases these periods have been creative or have been followed immediately by creative periods. It sometimes seems as if these minor breakdowns are necessary periods of readjustment; the required re-ordering of one's perceptions and faculties of vision must be preceded by a degree of disorder: disintegration is a necessary preliminary to re-integration and renewal. This was clearly the case with D. H. Lawrence and T. S. Eliot, for *The Waste Land* is clearly a turning point in his work. Theodore Roethke saw his own periods of disturbance as perhaps having this quality, but cried out in his notebook of 1954–58.

> I can't go on flying apart just for those who want the benefit of a few verbal kicks. My God, do you know what poems like that cost? They're not written vicariously: they come out of actual suffering, *real* madness.
>
> I've got to go beyond. That's all there is to it.
>
> Beyond what?
>
> The human, the human, you fool. Don't you see what I've done. I've come this far, and now I can't stop. It's too late, baby, it's too late.

The poet's difficulties are caused, as I have said, by external pressures, by the pressures of the environment, as well as by the damaging intensities of his vision. Society is not organized for poets. It is, indeed, organized in such a fashion as to make an alien of any person who finds it necessary to follow intuitions rather than regulations, to prize sensibility over social conformity, and to drop whatever he is doing in an instant if a poem beckons.

When Jeni Couzyn came to England from her native South Africa she found herself unable to fit into the social situation. She told me

... Well, I did a lot of jobs when I came to England, but I kept having nervous breakdowns in every job I did. They weren't so much breakdowns as break-ups. Everything fell apart because I couldn't blunt myself enough to cope ... Only now that I've been treating myself like a basket of eggs for some time have I begun to realize what things damage me and how to sort them out before I'm such a bloody mess that I'm lying on the floor. There's a poem in *Monkeys' Wedding* called *You Have To Say You Like It*, about what it's like to be utterly broken open and vulnerable, and it ends: 'The world was howling at her to rise, and say she liked it, and make a contribution.' When I realized that I couldn't grapple any more with the part of me that told me I ought to earn a living another part of me said, 'I'm not going to! I don't care!'

At that point Jeni Couzyn determined to work as a free-lance poet, and to earn her living by writing poems, giving poetry readings, and broadcasting. She refused to become part of the nine-to-five working world and she refused to do any work which she felt would be damaging to her. She told me

When I first started free-lancing I was starving—literally—I was found fainting on the floor of my flat many times. I remember going to see a neighbour once and asking him for some food, and the humiliation of it. I didn't know that people who are hungry feel ashamed. And I was so ashamed of being hungry all the time that I couldn't face any of my friends. He gave me some frozen chips. I didn't have any oil or butter of anything to fry them with. It didn't occur to me that I could have boiled them—I ate them raw. That was such an extremity and it lasted such a long time. . . . so I've become more interested in money; I've become interested in physical survival. And I've also become interested in having the right environment. I've realized how important it is to me that the people around me shouldn't be giving off bad vibrations, because if they are they destroy me. I've had to learn it, and I've had to learn the humiliation of accepting that I'm not tough.

Jeni Couzyn is still poor but she is no longer starving. She is not the only poet in this predicament today, and many poets would agree with her that they can only fit into the 'normal' social pattern at the risk of damaging or even destroying the only thing which gives life meaning.

As a consequence a number of poets live on various forms of welfare, or are supported financially by their wives, girl friends, or patrons. This is rarely satisfactory for inasmuch as the poet feels himself dependent upon the whim or the loyalty of someone else, he feels himself shackled, and develops, sooner or later, feelings of guilt or moods of unreasonable rebellion. Herbert Read once suggested that poets should take jobs which have nothing to do with literature or the arts, that they should do manual labour or work in factories so as to keep themselves clear of the dangers of using the language which is their poetic medium for baser tasks and thus blunting their sensibilities. Unfortunately many of those who followed his advice, or similar advice given by others, found the factory, or logging camp, or road-gang environment alien to the point of brutalizing them. They had no real way of talking to their fellows except by accepting their way of speech and their values as a norm in terms of which to live. During the nineteen fifties and sixties many poets took posts at Schools and Universities. In America posts of 'Writers in Residence' were created, and the poet was required to perform few duties, though usually obliged to teach at least one course of 'Creative Writing'. Some poets found, and still find, this employment congenial, as I do myself. Theodore Roethke was a brilliant teacher and enjoyed teaching very much. His notebooks contain many remarks on the way in which he regarded this task. 'Teaching' he noted, 'one of the few professions that permit love' and also 'One teaches out of love: it's an impertinence, an imposition, and in the end it's terrifying.' He also saw that there were dangers, however. He wrote of 'The damage of teaching: the constant contact with the undeveloped' and he revealed another danger when he wrote:

> To teach too intensively is to get so involved in particular psyches that there can be an actual loss of identity; destructive both to student and teacher. I remember a student saying, 'You carry us farther than we could ever go alone. Then when you're gone, it's too much to face.' Let's face it: much of this kind of teaching may perform the function of psychiatry, but it is absolutely fatal to proceed from such a premise or become self-conscious about what you're up to.

These are perhaps minor dangers. A more serious one is offered by the academic environment itself, for teachers of English Literature often seem to the poet to be attempting the destruction of poetry. Roethke again expresses what many poet-professors feel. He describes 'the Teaching Profession' as 'too many clever men without any gifts other than a low cunning; too many cardinal's secretaries'. He prays 'Dear Lord, may I never become one of those soft-faced sleek self-loving academic eunuchs, from whom all sharpness and cunning have fled, in self-created vacuity.' He pin-points 'A rat-trap sensibility' as one that 'slams down on a subject, maims and kills it but retains it'. He sums up 'The critics' attitude' as 'This poem exists for me to verbalize about it'. He goes far towards summing up many poets' feelings that basically the academic teachers of English Literature and the academic critics are simply parasitical forms by describing present day society as 'A culture in which it is easier to publish a book about poetry than a book of poems'. Roethke was not invariably temperate in his feelings or comments and his views may seem to some to be a little harsh. I can however state from my own experience that poets are not always regarded with affection or admiration by those who are being employed to inculcate a love and understanding of poetry in the young. I once spent twelve years teaching in the English Department of the University of Manchester. Never once in that twelve years did the University ask me to give a reading of my work, and one of my colleagues made it a habit of leaving the Staff Lounge whenever some incautious visitor committed the social gaffe of referring to my poetry. Although I was at that time the only member of that faculty who had published a book of poems of any kind (I published four collections during those years), I was never invited to meet any of those visiting poets whose visits I had not myself arranged. I found that this treatment did my work no good at all. I grew progressively depressed. It was not until I visited what was then Victoria College and the University of Massachusetts in 1963 that I became aware that it was socially acceptable to be a poet. I gave readings to large enthusiastic audiences and from that point on I had the confidence to develop new directions in my work. Roethke sums up my own conclusion when he writes, 'The artist needs, apparently, at least some appreciation of his work before he can effect the act of love.' 'All I need', another poet said once, and only partly in self-mockery, 'is adulation'. He meant that praise was not simply pleasurable but *necessary*. Without support a poet is likely to become trapped into an egoism that alone can give him a sense of purpose; he is obliged to provide his own claque.

Such egoism, however, leads finally to the negative euphoria of despair, and to destruction of one kind or another.

It may seem that I am basing my comments on the poet in academe upon very little evidence. I am, in fact, basing it upon twenty-three years' experience of universities in two continents and upon conversations with innumerable poets and poet-professors. It is common for a poet (or other writer, for that matter) to be refused promotion because he has not received a Ph.D., even though he has published a substantial amount of poetry or fiction or had his plays produced many times in professional, or semi-professional theatres. Had he written a laboured study of the poems of (let us say) William Shenstone he would have been rewarded by promotion, whereas his production of a book of poems far superior to those of Shenstone (which is not a difficult feat to accomplish) is regarded only as a not altogether amiable eccentricity. One well-known poet, after a year in a well-known college, swore to me 'I will never get into teaching again', and he was bitter not about the students but about the academic bureaucracy, the society in which he found himself. Too few academic careerists believe with Roethke that 'Teaching is an act of love, a spiritual cohabitation, one of the few sacred relationships left in a crass secular world', and all too many take what he calls 'the lazy man's out', which is to adopt the attitude 'I haven't read it: therefore it doesn't exist'.

Although I thus belabour Academe, I must, and do willingly, admit that the Universities may have saved far more poets than they have soured and that there are some Universities, many Universities, in which an influential minority of faculty and administration consider poetry to be a living art and regard it as essential to offer poets patronage and to give them the opportunity of transmitting something of their imaginative ardour and sensitivity to the young. Indeed the list of poets now teaching in Colleges and Universities is enormous, running at the last count, to well over three hundred names in the United States alone, and many of these Universities tolerate eccentricities that would cause the average business administration to turn white, reach for the pepto-bismol, and give the offending genius his cards. Nevertheless it would be stretching the truth to maintain that the Groves of Academe provide the ideal environment for any but a minority of poets who happen to be devoted to the art of teaching, and who have learned to blind themselves to the philistinism of their colleagues. This act of self-protective myopia, however, also has its snags. The young, eager and well-thought-of poets of the thirties and forties are now, all too often, the non-writing professors of the seventies. It would be discourteous to mention names but any reader that wishes can check up on the 'dead' poets who are now established academics and wonder whether or not their 'deaths' were truly inevitable.

I have spent so much time upon the poet in academe because most of today's poets are, or have been at one time, involved in teaching, and because it is important to show that even the apparently acceptable environment of literary studies can damage and disturb those poets who are sensitive enough to create the poems which take poetry into new territories.

Faced with these problems, those arising from the difficulty of coping with hypersensitivity itself and those arising from the conflict with society, the poet is inclined to seek some means to create a social group in which he can feel himself at home and by which his difficulties will be understood. He may also, if he is of a certain temperament, challenge society by inventing a social character for himself, and thus bully society into accepting him as a person demanding some kind of attention.

Some young poets have chosen to do this by deliberately becoming eccentrics. Louis MacNeice as an undergraduate wore a cloak and was conspicuously wayward in his social activities. Shelley took to carrying pistols and indulging in target practice. Yeats wore large floppy ties and a broadbrimmed hat. Others have dressed in kaftans, sported beards of strange cut, and indulged themselves with unusual pets. Gérard de Nerval promenaded Paris with a lobster on a string. Others have lavished their devotion upon panthers, pythons, and lion cubs. Aliens, outsiders, they have displayed their 'difference', and, by so doing, have not only challenged the society which wishes to ignore them, but also publicly advertised their opposition to the orthodoxies of the herd. The consequence of these manoeuvres is obvious. The poet becomes something of a notoriety, and is soon surrounded both by hangers-on and by other artists and poets who have recognized the signals he has been making. In this way many literary and artistic coteries develop, and while they may seem somewhat circus-like to the general public, they often provide their members with small social groups composed of people who are seriously concerned with the furtherance of art of one kind or another. There have been many such groups in the history of literature. Some have gathered around a magazine, such as T. S. Eliot's *Criterion*, Harold Monro's *Poetry Review*, Tambimuttu's *Poetry London*, and Eugene Jolas's *Transition*. Some have gathered around key personalities such as the Sitwells, Lady Ottoline Morell, and Leonard and Virginia Woolf.

Individual poets have often organized informal monthly, or weekly meetings, with other poets to discuss their work. G. S. Fraser and Edward Lucie Smith have both been involved in forming such groups. Sometimes these groups of like-minded people are dignified by critics and journalists with the names of 'Movements' or 'Schools'; in this century we have had the Bloomsbury school, the New Movement, The Beats, The Black Mountaineers, and even a group called simply 'The Group'.

All this points to the way in which the poet finds it necessary to counter his sense of alienation by discovering or inventing a society which will understand or at least tolerate his obsessive concern with making, and accept the intuitive and irrational aspects of his way of life as normal. It is ironic that the creation of these coteries tends to perpetuate that very feeling that poets, artists and writers are alien creatures which makes the coteries necessary.

By no means all poets choose, or are able, to involve themselves in social groups of the kind I have described, and by no means all choose to dress or act eccentrically. Wallace Stevens and T. S. Eliot were both reticent and conventional men in their social life. Herbert Read's solitary sartorial gesture towards his poethood was a bow tie, and only a minority of living poets attempt in any way to 'dress the part'. All, however, in one way or another, are obliged to find some way in which to 'belong'. In this they do not differ at all from the rest of humanity. Homo Sapiens is by nature gregarious. The only difference, indeed, is that the literary coterie, the poets' group, is composed of people who are otherwise solitaries. Most people have a social life of sorts connected with their work, whether it be on a factory floor, or in an office, or in one of the professions. They are continually dealing with people, feeling themselves to be part of a social whole. The poet, however, not only does his real work entirely alone, but, if he earns his bread in some other fashion, usually finds himself out of step with his colleagues. If he is not fortunate enough either to have a circle of fellow poets to reinforce his sense of vocation, or to find his non-poetic work sufficiently interesting to absorb a great deal of his energy, he is quite likely to discover that his poetic energy diminishes. Certainly it is notable that many poets who wrote both well and voluminously in their youth now write and publish very little, though they have become successful university teachers, publishers, journalists, and so forth. Some poets find it impossible to write when also working as a teacher. Basil Bunting has gone on record as saying that he cannot write in the periods he spends teaching poetry to students. Others have said the same. Norman Cameron blamed his work in an advertising agency for the waning of his poetic powers. John Wain found teaching so destructive that he left the University world to work as a free-lance writer. James Dickey, a successful business executive, resigned in order to devote all his time to writing and to giving poetry readings. Other poets have managed to live satisfactorily as poet-teachers or business men, of course. Wallace Stevens was a successful Insurance Executive. Theodore Roethke, Ivor Winters, John Berryman, Donald Davie, Tony Connor, David Wagoner, William Stafford, Randall Jarrell, J. V. Cunningham, Howard Nemerov, are or were all successful University teachers. The point, however, remains. Poets are obliged to be extremely careful in their choice of livelihood; a wrong choice can easily lead to the failure of their poetry or to the setting up of tensions which result in emotional or mental breakdown. It would be absurd to blame the suicides of Jarrell and Berryman upon their choice of Academe as a place of work, but it would not be absurd to suggest that to the strain inherent in being a poet at all they added the strain of being required to talk about poetry and the poetic process, knowing that they could never express the central mystery, and that, therefore, they were to some extent paltering with the truth.

That central mystery is indefinable. It can only be hinted at.

It has to do with those Muse visions I have discussed, with the poet's awareness of extra-sensory perceptions, with his profound sense of alienation (and hence, frequently, guilt), and with a burning and irrational conviction that (to use the words of Yeats), 'Words alone are certain good'. The poet himself cannot, however hard he tries, do more than touch upon some aspects of the heart of the creative process. He cannot generalize about his work with any ease, for he is constantly being surprised by the way it comes into being. He can only, with a stubborn tenacity which has to be characteristic of anyone who is to write poetry for more than a brief period of adolescence, continue making poems. Occasionally he may be able to describe something about the genesis of a particular poem, but for the most part he feels that the only medium in which he can communicate more than hazardous approximations is poetry itself. Only poetry can explain poetry or interpret poetry. He is, as it were, fettered by the very language which makes him free. That which provides his vision is that which prevents him ever being able to explain it. This is perhaps the greatest frustration and alienation of all; while critics write about his verse, reviewers praise (or condemn) it, and teachers place it on syllabuses, he is unable ever to agree or disagree with their views, or enter into anything resembling a serious discussion, for they are, to him, speaking a different language. They are talking of poetry as if it were something he knows it not to be. He can only recall the experience of poetry and be silent, or bide his time until he has an opportunity to describe, without too great a sense of inadequacy, the way one or two poems came to him, in the hope that some will understand. What most people seem incapable of understanding, among other things, is that poetry is not merely a craft but a way of life, and one which is peculiarly demanding. The poet when in a creative period often finds himself involved in a kind of continuous dialogue with his Muse, his Daimon, and is obliged to seize every opportunity to attend to this developing conversation. This, Kathleen Raine told me, is why one cannot write poems just in the odd five minutes between giving one's attention to some other thing.

It has to be an uninterrupted reverie and one may do manual work during that time but one has not to be interrupted by extraneous adventitious mental tasks. I've always written best when alone; I have to get away by myself for a spell and listen to the Daimon and sometimes it takes some time to get back and of course the intervals get longer and longer and, as you know, I'm so taken up now with family obligations that it's impossible for me to make this relationship with the Daimon at the present time. But the last volume I wrote was last year and at that time I think all the poems were written in the early morning, not from dream material, but in that state of suspended being that one has between waking and the day and its obligations coming in on one. And in the morning—it's quite true—one wakes up with ideas that have been put into one's mind during sleep, at which time one is nearer the unconscious.

I asked Kathleen Raine how it was possible to gear one's life to this necessity to listen to the Daimon. She said:

I remember Alexis Leger saying that one must never forget that being a poet is a way of life and that it is a total way of life. He, I am sure, never allowed any human relationship to interrupt his inner reverie.

Which points to a certain ruthlessness, doesn't it?

Well, aren't all poets ruthless?

I think they are, yes.

After all, you are either ruthless to—you must be ruthless to something and if you are permissive to human relationships you are being ruthless to your poetry, and forbidding it to flower and be born, and it's a

193

matter of what you regard as the more important. And of course for a true poet it seems to me that you must put nothing before your vocation, and this is very hard for a woman.

It's very hard for a man. It's not easy for anybody.

I suppose so. You have to have a great certainty, and a great integrity, and, of course, no one helps you.

How do you hang on to that great certainty? I remember the certainty I felt when I was a young bad poet, but now I am a middle-aged slightly better poet the certainty keeps disappearing.

Well, of course you may lose the title to the certainty through neglecting your task, and there is the myth of Bellerophon who rode Pegasus and at a certain time Pegasus threw him and he wouldn't come to him again. And this is an ever-present danger—the fact that one has been called to be a poet once doesn't say that one can neglect one's vocation for half a lifetime and that it will still be there. You must remain open; you must continue to be a poet; you must dedicate yourself to it for a lifetime. I may now have let it go almost too long from what has seemed to me the obligations of my situation.
It can always happen and one must always remember that it can happen. Not everyone who might have been a poet has continued and fulfilled themselves. We always have the possibility of failing. We may fail. This is always possible.

What must one do not to be thrown by Pegasus?

'Thou shalt have no other gods before me!' It doesn't matter what. You can put anything before your poetry and that will be quite sufficient to destroy it. It may be the most high-sounding things like family obligations—one must put one's children before one's work—well, in that case perhaps one shouldn't have married and had children. There are a thousand times in the day, let alone in the life, when one can make the wrong choice. And most of us do many times. So that I think to say 'Well, look at the situation I am in, you know. I've got this and that obligation'—you must ask yourself at what point you took on those obligations and whether in fact you should have done so.

Finally, the poet must be a responsible person. He may appear to be an exceptional kind of person, but he is only exceptional really in the way that members of any other profession are exceptional. While he may legitimately complain about the poor working conditions and the derisive financial rewards which society affords him, he should not demand that he be given privileged treatment. All too often young poets assume that, because they are poets, the world owes them a sinecure. I do not believe it. I believe only that the world owes them proper attention and proper courtesy. Hart Crane, in writing to Yvor Winters, made several good points. He said:

> I'm all too ready to concede that there are several other careers more engaging to follow than that of poetry. But the circumstances of one's birth, the conduct of one's parents, the current economic structure of society, and a thousand other local factors have as much or more to say about successions to such occupations, the naive volitions of the poet to the contrary. I agree with you, of course, that the poet should in as large a measure as possible adjust himself to society. But the question will remain as to how far the conscience is justified in compromising with the age's demands.[1]

Later in the same letter he said:

> I have a certain code of ethics. I have not as yet attempted to reduce it to any exact formula, and if I did I should probably embark on an endless tome with monthly additions and digressions every year. It seems obvious that a certain decent marriage and action is a paramount requirement in any poet, deacon or carpenter. And though I reserve myself the pleasant right to define these standards in a somewhat individual way, and to shout and complain when circumstances against me seem to warrant it, on the other hand I believe myself to be speaking honestly when I say that I have never been able to regret—for long—whatever has happened to me, more especially those decisions which at times have been permitted a free will. (Don't blame me entirely for bringing down all this simplicity on your head—your letter almost solicits it !) And I am as completely out of sympathy with the familiar whimpering caricature of the artist and his 'divine rights' as you seem to be. I am not a Stoic, though I think I could learn more in that direction if I came to (as I may sometime) appreciate more highly the imaginative profits of such a course.[2]

W. S. Graham wrote:

> Let us say that I'm a poet. Is a poet in any way special ? Yes, but only in that he is concerned with putting into words those sudden desolations and happiness that descend on us uninvited there where we each are within our lonely rooms never really entered by anybody else and from which we never really emerge. Therefore he shouldn't be a freak

---

[1] Brom Weber (ed.), *The Complete Poems and Selected Letters and Prose of Hart Crane*. Oxford University Press 1968, pp. 241–242.

[2] ibid., pp. 243–244.

or a decoration of society thinking himself exempt from normal standards of behaviour, not able to boil an egg, and imagining society owes him something. When we hear the word POET we reach for our drink. For most people think of a poet as a third lazy, a third phoney and a third organically eccentric and no wonder. No, he should be even more responsible and have less need to win the thousand little battles of the moment which occur in conversation. He should be too concerned with honesty to worry about being right.

To finish this evangelical editorial, it is not enough remembered that a poet is an ordinary man like any other man here to make his brief gesture of joy before he goes, and his behaviour, apart from the making of poetry, is subject to the same measurements.[1]

In the context of the difficulties I have been outlining in this chapter, neither Hart Crane nor W. S. Graham are asking for 'special treatment', and neither has seen fit to claim that their work presents any over-all overmastering perspective upon the total human predicament. They have left it to the critics to perceive what they may of the unity their work forms and of its drive towards a poetic philosophy, a total vision of the human scene. Most poets, indeed, do not choose to counter the general belief that poets are creatures operating in terms of unconnected spasms of perception. In our century only Robert Graves and W. B. Yeats have put forward a prose description of the system of thought, belief, and perception within which their poetry moves and upon which it depends for its ultimate coherence. Indeed one of the things which poets find it most difficult to explain is their sense that every word they write in poetry is part of a whole, not always clearly seen but always, however dimly, apprehended. Shy of appearing to take over the territory of the speculative philosopher, they do not wish to suggest, except by the way in which their poems add together, that they are involved in an onward moving drive towards an ever increasing understanding of man's place in the universe. They avoid expressions of their credo, being (like Keats) averse to presenting opinion, but certain of experience, and hopeful that the experience of their poems may lead the reader to detect, perhaps even more clearly than they themselves, the over-all pattern in which the personal and the universal mesh and interrelate, and in which the temporary and the eternal come to terms with each other.

Jeni Couzyn, who is not an ostensibly philosophical poet, and who is certainly no academic, is typical in that she has nowhere attempted in print to express her sense of the whole pattern which subsumes her

[1] *Promenade* No. 66. Cheltenham 1965, p. 2.

individual poems. She did, however, when I tackled her on the subject present a credo that, in its symbolic thinking and its comprehensive range, reveals clearly the way in which the poet regards his individual poems as being expressions of, and implications of, a wider view. She told me

For me it's as if the mind is a geographical landscape. The intellect is a little garden and that's where you live, and that's where your house is and that's *walled*, and it's got a gate. There you're in total control. *You* plant the flowers. *You* choose the flowers you want to grow. *You* choose the trees. *You* prune them. *You* make all the decisions and everything is governed by *your* will and your vision. *You* govern that garden. *You* cultivate it. If you don't want to cultivate it, if you're bone idle, it's full of weeds and disordered. It reflects totally *your* will.

Outside that garden is the Wild Country. And there there's mist and there's cliffs and there's waterfalls and there's rivers and there's chasms and there's mountains and there's moors and there's deserts, and that Wild Country is your personal experience. You're not in control. What happens to you, happens. You can say 'I choose to walk along this beautiful quiet country lane called Marriage where everything is going to be easy for me'. You can choose the path, but you can't choose when there's going to be a lightning storm or when the locusts are going to attack that country and literally sweep it barren in five minutes as locusts could. You're not in control. That for me is your personal experience of your emotions, of everything that happens to you in your life. The main thing is that your will isn't governing it. Things happen, and you see them and you choose whether to withdraw or advance, but it's hazardous. The ultimate territory beyond the Wild Country is the Ocean, and in that Ocean territory what's true for you is in some form true for every single live thing in the Universe. When you get to Ocean territory you're in touch with what a flower feels and what a human being feels; you're in touch with the evolution of the plant and the person and the planet.

I believe that everything that is true in ocean territory is true at every level. It is true as a whole and in every part of the whole. In the Garden nothing is true; everything is created. In the Wild Country things are just true within that context. But in Ocean territory things are true at every level, ultimately true. A lot of poets walk along the cliff edge because it appears to put one in touch, but that is false. It's not true at all levels. It's only partly true. It's cliff-edge poetry. To me it's a false source. For me the true poem is a poem that is true not only for everybody but for everything. I have a moment in my best poems when I actually know that I have broken through from the Wild

Country into Ocean territory. And I *know* it, you know! There's no doubt!

I asked Jeni Couzyn how she felt about the view that poets should explore their perceptions to the very brink, the edge of what is controllable. She said

> People who have been damaged by the external trappings of their life have been thrown off the edge, or been very near to the edge, and that has made it possible for them to have no walls, and having no walls has made it possible for them to hear the distant drummer. But the Ocean Territory is not what is on the other side of the edge. On the other side of the edge is the Abyss. It's just damage; it's just death; it's just destruction. A lot of people write that kind of 'edge poetry'. It's a cliff edge and a waterfall; it's not the Ocean. The Ocean is ordered and infinite, but the Edge is Death. Poets who deliberately walk near the edge are writing from a false source. The edge most poets walk along is a shattering of all they hold most dear. They often do it by being promiscuous, or living in some way dangerously. They take a risk and they get a false kind of electricity from that risk. If there's a strike of lightning it's at once dangerous and beautiful, and a charge of electricity, of energy, but if there's a true source of current then it's constant and well ordered. The Edge to me is the lightning; the Ocean is the current, the source.

I asked her how all this related to notions of individual immortality and reincarnation, for many poets believe in both these things. She said

> I think Christianity caused more trouble than anything else because Christianity preaches all the time the individual soul, the eternal existence of the individual soul. We're like leaves on a tree. We think we're individuals, but if we stand back a little we can see that we're each a leaf, an individual leaf on a total tree, and we might fall down one by one when the winter is coming, and we might come out one by one when the spring is coming, and we might each look a bit different. We have our own individual life, but we're just part of the tree if you step back a bit. And if you step back farther you see that the tree is part of the wood. And if you step back farther still you see that the wood is part of the earth and if then you step back you see that the earth's part of the galaxy. You cannot separate it.
>
> To me it's very clear that life changes its form but is not destroyed. The one mistake that so many mystics seem to me to make is to assume that if something happens after death to one particular saint or prophet or ghost or villain then it happens in every case. I do believe that a human soul can go from one life into a next without dispersing

into some other stream of energy but I think it's most unlikely that it happens in general. It's such a limited view, Reincarnation. Life is *one thing*. It's like water. That's why I use this word Ocean all the time. You can put it into as many different vessels as you like. You can put it into cups, jugs, vases, bottles—anything you like—different sizes, shapes—but all the time it's *water*. It is part of the one thing which is *water*.

She suggested that when a person 'remembers' an earlier life that person may have become aware of life as a whole and have sensed his or her oneness with it and then identified with a particular aspect of it. On the other hand she agreed that some people might really have been other people in a different life, but thought it more likely that the individual life was divided among a number of life forms. She repeated her dislike of Christian doctrine, saying

It's incredible to me that Christians for all this time have believed that Eternal Paradise could be the survival of your individual soul. To me the boundaries of being an individual are nothing but pain. My boundaries are pain, and freedom from pain is freedom from my individual boundaries.

Andrew Marvell in the two opening stanzas of his *A Dialogue between the Soul and Body* expresses with miraculous power the soul's resentment of the boundaries of the individual life and the body's resentment of the soul. It is interesting to notice that the 'edge' of Jeni Couzyn's analysis has an equivalent in Marvell's 'Precipice'

Soul

O who shall, from this Dungeon, raise
A Soul inslav'd so many wayes?
With bolts of Bones, that fetter'd stands
In Feet; and manacled in Hands.
Here blinded with an Eye; and there
Deaf with the drumming of an Ear.
A Soul hung up, as 'twere, in Chains
Of Nerves, and Arteries, and Veins.
Tortur'd, besides each other part,
In a vain Head, and double Heart.

Body

O who shall me deliver whole,
From bonds of this Tyrannic Soul?
Which, stretcht upright, impales me so,
That mine own Precipice I go;

And warms and moves this needless Frame:
(A Fever could but do the same.)
And, wanting where its spight to try,
Has made me live to let me dye.
A Body that could never rest,
Since this ill Spirit it possest.

Much of the striving of Theodore Roethke was to escape individuality into a perception and expression of the total life force, to become one with the 'evolution of the plant and the person and the planet'. The risks he took were not the willed risks of the seeker after adventitious electrical excitements. On the other hand it seems that in many poems Robert Lowell, Sylvia Plath, and Anne Sexton, whose breakdowns have all been publicly admitted, appear to be rather attempting to re-order individual memories, and make sense of personal obsessions than to explore towards the universal. Lowell's most recent poetry in particular appears to be autobiographical in a quite narrow sense, and the speaker of the poems does not register as in any way typical of human experience as a whole. Are we, then, to condemn Lowell for not leading us to the universal, and reserve our praise for the more universal vision of Roethke, and for the philosophical visions of Edwin Muir, Kathleen Raine, and the Platonist poets ? Should a poet—and this is perhaps the heart of the matter—consider all his trials and tribulations useless if they do not lead him to the presentation of a universal vision ? Jeni Couzyn said:

I don't think that the poet must necessarily be able to tell people the big truths. He needn't be able to tell them about the Ocean. For example if they are the sun-spot on the leaf the poet could perhaps tell them about the veins in the leaf and the branches and perhaps the tree, and that might be enough. It is not necessary that he should know about the whole wood and the whole earth and the whole universe to be able to say something meaningful for that sun on that one leaf. To me, to be able to tell about the veins on the leaf and the branches on the tree is a great deal. The partial truth, putting people in touch with each other and putting them in touch with their own time—that's important ! And that's what poets do, not by telling people but by singing people, singing so the people can hear.

The poet is not always telling people or singing *to* people; he is simply 'singing so the people can hear'. Kathleen Raine told me

I remember Ezra Pound when I went to see him in St Elizabeths. The friend who took me told me as we went away, 'You know, I asked Ezra "Who do you write for, Ezra, finally ?" and he said "Well, I

Suppose GOD''' and I think one does write the truth—the best truth one knows to the best of one's ability as really and exactly as possible; one doesn't write for an audience, but one writes in the faith that there are other human beings like oneself. Perhaps the greatest honour one can do other human beings is to suppose one's own deepest thoughts are not unknown to one's fellow men. This is a more honourable attitude to one's fellow human beings than thinking one must write simply in order to be understood by the working-class or whatever it may be, or by the young.

It is of course those 'deepest thoughts' which matter most and which justify the poet's labours. One must, in writing poetry, be dealing always with what Kathleen Raine called 'living thought, the living mind-stuff of the universe'. She added:

> If one tries to be a poet without doing so, of course one is purely academic; one is simply writing an imitation of poetry which it is very easy to do if you're well trained in the English Schools. There's lots of it. Some of it is very ingenious, but it isn't what you and I mean by poetry.

It is, perhaps, difficult to draw a line between that important poetry of 'partial truth' and that non-poetry of academic ingenuity which so often masquerades as poetry in the pages of our periodicals, and is criticized as poetry by those academic critics who prefer a puzzle to a paean and wit to wonderment. Those who spend their lives on 'partial' poetry may be honest and dedicated poets, and if they are so they may find themselves occasionally in hazard. Those who devote themselves to the creation of academic non-poetry are unlikely, unless they have additional psychological problems, to face the stresses of the true poet, and may easily escape scot-free into literary nullity. They are liable, however, to be a nuisance to the poets proper. There is no one so intolerant of poetry as a failed poet, and no one so desperately destructive of imaginative endeavours as one whose creative powers have been allowed to die from misuse or neglect. As Roethke points out:

> Who think in symbols, naturally, as the mad do, as children do, have a hard time with those fierce sweaty tin-eared logicians who bring to the work of the imagination all the sensibility of a shoe-clerk. But it's in this area that progress must be made. To them there's no logic of the imagination, no place for the suddenly right made irrelevance, no time or reason for the mind to stretch loose and shrink: no time, in a word, for poetry, an art they pay lip-service to (provided it is in the past).

It is the arrogance as well as the insensitivity and ignorance of such as these which depresses the poet. For all that some have said, poets are rarely arrogant. They may be proud of some of their work, but they know that they themselves were 'given' the greater part of all that is best in their writings. They do not boast of their emotional difficulties or claim 'special status' because of them; they do not regard themselves as martyrs, but as people who have to accept the difficulties that go along with the job. Though aware—often uncomfortably aware—of having powers of perception and even magical abilities which appear to be uncommon, they do not believe that these set them apart but rather suspect that other people have simply not come to terms with faculties that all possess. Jeni Couzyn said:

> I don't think that poets are anything special; I think it's very important to say that. Other people than poets can be in touch in their own way with that which is beyond their specific boundaries. That's all a poet is doing—getting in touch with that beyond himself. Probably almost all human beings do it.

Jeni Couzyn may be correct in this, but non-artists tend, I believe, to 'get in touch with that beyond themselves' only at random or on special occasions, at times of intense emotion. The poet is one who devotes his whole life to this activity, and does so in the teeth of social opposition or, at best, indifference, and despite much emotional and mental disturbance. He must be very strong if he is to continue for a whole lifetime, and he must tell himself over and over again, for few others will tell him, that the job is worth doing. He must, in humility, revering the vocation itself and not the follower of the vocation, follow Theodore Roethke's advice to himself:

Remind yourself once more of the absolute holiness of your task.

Conclusion

I have spent a great deal of time discussing the difficulties of the poet, for it seems to me that these are little understood, while a poet's successes, his fame, his Pulitzer prizes, his world-wide reputation, are matters of common knowledge. I have tried indeed, to present rather the private than the public character of the poet. Although the difficulties I have outlined are real and ever-present, in recent years it has become much easier than before for poets to surmount all but their most inward problems. Some poets in North America and in England contrive to earn a living very largely by giving readings of their work. A well-known poet in the United States has little difficulty in getting $500.00 for one reading. Some poets receive as much as $1200.00 for a day spent in giving a reading and discussing their work in a seminar. In England the BBC has for years been a substantial patron of living poets, as has the CBC in Canada, and the British Arts Council, like the Canada Council and the American National Endowment of the Arts programme, assists individual poets with grants and supports publishing ventures which enable poets to be published and be paid for their work. Moreover, many Boards of Education in different parts of the English Speaking World are alive to the educational possibilities of having real live poets visit schools, and some School Districts in North America have organized poetry-circuits.

The poet is, therefore, less likely to starve or be obliged to live on welfare than he was some years ago. Nevertheless, not all good poets are good performers, and this is unfortunate. It seems indeed, nowadays, that society demands of the poet that he should also be something of an actor, should be able to 'project' his poetry to an audience. This leads, and has led, to some poets writing work which sounds well, but reads badly on the page. Tony Connor says that he likes to make poems which demand to be spoken aloud, but is careful to ensure that they also have presence when printed. Other poets have been, and are, less careful, and some feel quite strongly that the *real* poem is the performed poem rather than the written one, which they regard only as a 'text' or poetical 'score'. The widespread appreciation of poetry readings, of jazz and poetry concerts, and of poetry and rock performances, has resulted in the production of a great deal of high-sounding but intellectually and imaginatively null verbiage. Some poets find this situation depressing, believing in a kind of poetic Greshams Law that 'bad poetry drives out good'. I do not myself feel this to be the case. I believe rather that those young people who nowadays think the attending of poetry readings a quite usual and pleasurable activity, are likely to find their tastes maturing as they mature, and to become readers of or listeners to more significant work. I also feel that the increasing amount of general acceptance of poetry as a part of the world of leisure entertainment must lead to a healthier attitude towards both poets and poems. It may be, indeed, that the young (especially in North America) are at last leading us towards a society in which poets may not feel totally alien. I therefore welcome the poetry readings in pubs, the ill-printed broadsheets of poems by near-illiterate hopefuls, the softly groaning street-singers of original songs, and all those aspects of what has been called the sub-culture and the underground, which tend to treat poets and poetry with interest and respect but without that undue reverence which so often is a disguise for deep distrust.

I have mentioned the ill-printed broadsheets of some of the hopeful young. What about the established publishers ? Here the situation has not improved at all over the last two decades. It has, indeed, worsened. Few of the big publishers accept poetry, and when they do they usually fail to give it adequate distribution. A few poets receive good treatment; the majority do not. It is common for publishers to either refuse or (more usually) 'forget' to ensure that copies of a poet's books are on sale at a place when he is giving a reading there. It has reached so bad a state that many poets now buy their own books from the publisher and act as their own retailers while travelling the land, for otherwise their audience may never get to see their poems in print. Booksellers (with some justification) object to this, but they should not object too strongly; they too do little to support poetry, with some notable exceptions.

The consequence of this situation is that nowadays very few poets and a lessening number of poetry readers pay much attention to the publishers name on a book of poems. Some poets actually prefer to have their books issued by small lively firms who have a limited distribution service but who use that service to the full, rather than by large and so-called prestigious firms who do not seem to get the books out to the bookshops, libraries or campus bookstores. A few publishers do attempt to publicize and distribute their books of poems and even go so far as to organize reading tours for their authors; these are in a tiny minority. I have heard many poets on both sides of the Atlantic saying, during the last two years, that they are abandoning the 'ordinary' kind of publication and having their work issued only by small presses. Poets are disinclined to do battle with big bureaucratic machines, and detest the impersonality of the mammoth publishing empire, almost as much as they detest the self-congratulatory and patronizing tone in which so many publishers' editors speak to them of their work.

Horror stories about poets and publishers are, of course, legion. Poets fail to understand why it is that publishers do not simply *try* to sell books of poems. It baffles them. The average publisher simply rests on the dictum 'Poetry Does not Sell!' and ignores the evidence of many thousands attending poetry readings every month in North America, a proportion of whom always buy the performers' books when they are given the opportunity. Moreover publishers, and those other entrepreneurs whom one may group together under the general blurred heading of 'the Media' have of recent years, tended to require instant success of their authors. I know many cases in which a poet has been told 'Your last book didn't sell sufficiently well to justify us taking another'; I am tempted to remind such people that it is not the first or even the second blow of the pickaxe which reveals the gold. In other times publishers tended to accept the work of an author in whom they had faith and continue to publish him just as long as they did not lose more than a tiny amount; now the average publisher thinks otherwise, sometimes because he is part of a huge and tyrannical system, and sometimes because he is success-orientated to the point of frenzy. Theodore Roethke reflected grimly:

> Today there's no time for the mistakes of a long and slow development: dazzle or die. Would Yeats' career be possible in this country today?

I also am reminded of e. e. cummings continuing the title of his collection of poems, *No Thanks*, with the dedication

TO
Farrar & Rinehart
Simon & Schuster
Coward McCann
Limited Editions
Harcourt, Brace
Random House

Equinox Press
Smith & Haas
Viking Press
Knopf
Dutton
Harper's
Scribner's
Covici, Friede

all of whom had rejected the collection, though cummings was by that time an established poet with five earlier volumes to his credit.

This example of the difficulties of a middle-aged poet—cummings was forty-one years old when *No Thanks* was published in 1935—is not unusual. Since I began planning this book some years ago I have heard of many similar cases. I do not wish to mention names as the poets concerned might feel that an account of their difficulties could damage their standing in the eyes of those who consider poetry must be judged as a popularity contest. It seems clear, however, that the middle-aged poet who has received no major awards or prizes and who has remained unblessed by personal notoriety but who has, quite simply, been writing well and steadily for a number of years, may receive the respect of his peers but is unlikely to be given the support accorded the young whose promise is new and whose mettle is untested by time.

There are of course exceptions to this role for there are some exceptional publishers. There are men dedicated to publishing quality books as poets are dedicated to poetry. One can only regret that, in both instances, there are not more of them.

The poet has now, however, other fish to fry. He is able (if he is sufficiently well-known or well-connected) to issue recordings of his work on disc or tape and these products are slowly beginning to form a more significant part of the culture, though it is odd to reflect that two of the pioneers of this kind of poetry publishing were poets as different from each other as John Masefield and Lawrence Ferlinghetti.

All this, of course, relates more to the poet's 'career' as a public figure, to his social role, than to his poethood and his pursuit of his solitary vision. That vision, however, depends for its sustenance upon the assurance he is given by society that he is getting his message across, that he is not simply speaking to an empty auditorium. It is particularly important that the young should not suffer this isolation, this alienation, and become the 'mute inglorious Miltons' the Elegist mourned. Whatever the Dow Jones listings may say, we need our poets. They provide us not only with entertainment in the broadest sense (Why should John Wayne be more rewarded than John Wain ?) but also enable us to see ourselves and understand our place in the universe feelingly, not merely objectively. Indeed there is now a growing realization that the writing of poetry may be as valid a form of therapy for emotionally disturbed people as the long-established art therapy, for not all disturbed people are visually orientated and can be helped with paint or pencil, or tactile and able to express themselves and reorder their disturbances in clay; some are verbal and need to scribble. It may be, indeed, that poetry has always been, from the days of magical incantations and war-cries, something of a tribal therapy, as well as a vehicle for history, religion, propaganda, and the most intense kinds of human insight.

It is not, however, my business in this book, even at its conclusion, to attempt a definition of the value and utility of poetry. I have only been concerned to attempt to answer that question 'What is it like to be a poet ?' and to answer it as fully as I can. I am aware that my report has been a highly selective one; it could not be anything else, for I am myself involved in poetry and have been since I was a small child. Nevertheless, if what I have said only serves to arouse discussion, and to bring the question of the role of the poet today into people's minds, this book will not have been entirely useless.

Appendix

A Moment of Eternity
To George Ogilvie

The great song ceased
—Aye, like a wind was gone,
And our hearts came to rest,
Singly as leaves do,
And every leaf a flame.

My shining passions stilled
Shone in the sudden peace
Like countless leaves
Tingling with the quick sap
Of Immortality.

I was a multitude of leaves
Receiving and reflecting light,
A burning bush
Blazing for ever unconsumed,
Nay, ceaselessly,
Multiplying in leaves and light
And instantly
Burgeoning in buds of brightness,
—Freeing like golden breaths
Upon the cordial air
A thousand new delights,
—Translucent leaves
Green with the goodness of Eternity,
Golden in the Heavenly light,
—The golden breaths
Of my eternal life,
Like happy memories multiplied,
Shining out instantly from me
And shining back for ever into me,
—Breaths given out
But still unlost,
For ever mine

In the infinite air,
The everlasting foliage of my soul
Visible awhile
Like steady and innumerable flames,
Blending into one blaze
Yet each distinct
With shining shadows of difference.

A sudden thought of God's
Came like a wind
Ever and again
Rippling them as waters over stars,
And swiftlier fanning them
And setting them a-dance,
Upflying, fluttering down,
Moving in orderly intricacies
Of colour and of light,
Delaying, hastening,
Blazing and serene,
Shaken and shining in the turning wind,
Lassoing cataracts of light
With rosy boughs,
Or clamouring in echoing unequalled heights,
Rhythmical sprays of many-coloured fire
And spires chimerical
Gleaming in fabulous airs,
And suddenly
Lapsing again
To incandescence and increase.

And again the wind came
Blowing me afar
In fair fantastic fires,
—Ivies and irises invading
The upland garths of ivory;
Queen daisies growing
In the tall red grass
By pools of perfect peace;
And bluebells tossing
In transparent fields;
And silver airs
Lifting the crystal sources in dim hills
And swinging them far out like bells of glass
Pealing pellucidly
And quivering in faery flights of chimes;

Shivers of wings bewildered
In alleys of virgin dream;
Floral dances and revels of radiance
Whirling in stainless sanctuaries;
And eyes of Seraphim,
Shining like sunbeams on eternal ice,
Lifted toward the unexplored
Summits of Paradise.
And the wind ceased.

Light dwelt in me,
Pavilioned there.
I was a crystal trunk,
Columnar in the glades of Paradise,
Bearing the luminous boughs
And foliaged with the flame
Of infinite and gracious growth,
—Meteors for roots,
And my topmost spires
Notes of enchanted light
Blind in the Godhead!
—White stars at noon!

I shone within my thoughts
As God within us shines.

And the wind came,
Multitudinous and light
I whirled in exultations inexpressible
—An unpicturable, clear,
Soaring and glorying,
Swift consciousness,
A cosmos turning like a song of spheres
On apices of praise,
A separate colour,
An essential element and conscious part
Of successive and stupendous dreams
In God's own heart!
And the wind ceased
And like a light I stood,
A flame of glorious and complex resolve,
Within God's heart.

I knew then that a new tree,
A new tree and a strange,
Stood beautifully in Heaven.

I knew that a new light
Stood in God's heart
And a light unlike
The Twice Ten Thousand lights
That stood there,
Shining equally with me,
And giving and receiving increase of light
Like the flame that I was
Perpetually.
And I knew that when the wind rose
This new tree would stand still
Multiplied in light but motionless,
And I knew that when God dreamt
And His creative impulses
Ran through us like a wind
And we flew like clear and coloured
Flames in His dreams,
(Adorations, Gratitudes, and Joys,
Plenary and boon and pure,
Crystal and burning-gold and scarlet
Competing and co-operating flames
Reflecting His desires,
Flashing like epical imaginings
And burning virgin steeps
With ceaseless swift apotheoses)
One light would stand unmoved.

And when on pinnacles of praise
All others whirled
Like a white light deeper in God's heart
This light would shine,
Pondering the imponderable,
Revealing ever clearlier
Patterns of endless revels,
Each gesture freed,
Each shining shadow of difference,
Each subtle phase evolved
In the magnificent and numberless
Revelations of ecstasy
Succeeding and excelling inexhaustibly,
—A white light like a silence
Accentuating the great songs !
—A shining silence wherein God
Might see as in a mirror
The miracles that He must next achieve !

Ah, Light,
That is God's inmost wish,
His knowledge of Himself,
Flame of creative judgment,
God's interrogation of infinity,
Searching the unsearchable,
—Silent and steadfast tree
Housing no birds of song,
Void to the wind,
But rooted in God's very self,
Growing ineffably,
Central in Paradise !

When the song ceased
And I stood still,
Breathing new leaves of life
Upon the eternal air,
Each leaf of all my leaves
Shone with a new delight
Murmuring Your name.

O Thou,
Who art the wisdom of the God
Whose ecstasies we are!

HUGH MACDIARMID

Index of Names

213

Index of Names